HORSE TALKS

Lectures and Lecturing Techniques
for Students and Instructors

by

MAXINE CAVE BHSSM+T

J. A. ALLEN
London

British Library Cataloguing in Publication Data
A catalogue record for this book is available from the British Library

ISBN 0.85131.596.8

Published in Great Britain in 1994 by
J. A. Allen & Company Limited,
1, Lower Grosvenor Place, Buckingham Palace Road,
London, SW1W 0EL.

Typeset in Hong Kong by Setrite Typesetters Ltd.
Printed in Hong Kong by Dau Hua Printing Co. Ltd.

Illustrations by Maggie Raynor
Designed by Nancy Lawrence

Contents

Introduction

The aim of this book is to provide sound theoretical knowledge of horse care and management, together with an outline of the practical skills required. The practical skills should be developed through "hands-on" experience, with guidance from a qualified instructor, as there is no substitute for practical work.

I have covered a range of subjects in enough depth to provide any horse person with the necessary knowledge to care for a variety of horses and ponies in different work. Students taking the British Horse Society Stages I and II examinations will find all the required stable management subjects covered here.

Trainers and students can use the book together or individually. Ideally, students should read through each lecture in advance. The trainer can then deliver the lecture, concentrating on the practical skills and checking and confirming the students' knowledge as appropriate.

By following this method, there should be little or no need for students to take notes, as the written lecture can be used for reference. This enables students to give the trainer their full attention while the lecture is being delivered.

All that is needed is a good instructor and a suitable location in which to demonstrate the practical skills.

1 Lecturing Techniques

Preparation

Good preparation is the key to a successful lecture. If you are poorly prepared you will not instil confidence in the students, and their attention will wander at an early stage. Read the preparation notes that precede each lecture, along with the notes on timing, resources and location, to ensure that you are properly organised. You can then begin the lecture with confidence.

Aims and Objectives

Students will be more attentive if they understand why they need to know about each subject. A good introduction will explain the purpose of your talk/demonstration. The aims and objectives that are set out at the beginning of each lecture may be used as the introduction.

The less-experienced lecturer should consider reading from the text or writing down their introduction in order to be certain of starting with a confident delivery.

Timing

The amount of time available will dictate how much of each subject you can cover per session. By making a time plan you are more likely to keep to the subject and not allow yourself to be sidetracked. Some subjects will need to be broken down into many small sections. This allows for breaks, which may be quite short, for coffee, questions, etc., or may form a good cut-off point for that day. The lecture could then be resumed at a suitable time, for example the next day.

Time plans can help you to be flexible without losing sight of your goal. There are many occasions when students' questions, or their ability to grasp a subject, may lead you off on a tangent. It is important to answer these questions and to check the students' understanding, but having done this you can then return to your original plan, knowing exactly how much extra time you need to complete that subject.

In the following lectures, I have assessed the time needed on the assumption that the students already have some prior knowledge of the subject. You will need to take more time if the subject is completely new to the students, or if they have any type of learning difficulties.

Resources

Resources include anything that will aid the delivery of the lecture. Your choice of resources will obviously be governed by what is available to you but will also depend upon the size of group being lectured to and their experience and age group. When making your choice, you should bear in mind that you are more likely to keep the attention of the students, and make a lasting impression with your lecture, if you aim to stimulate as many of the five senses as possible. With a little thought, many horse-related subjects can incorporate hearing, seeing, touching, smelling and sometimes tasting. Too many lectures rely on hearing alone, with groups of students listening to the lecturer for long periods. This often leads to loss of concentration due to a lack of stimuli.

1. Locations

Choose your location carefully; it will make a tremendous difference to the students' ability to concentrate. Students will be uncomfortable and may fidget or even fall asleep if the room is either too cold or too hot. The same problem will result from inappropriate seating and tables. Constant interruptions, perhaps from people coming into the room, from noises or from activity outside the window, distract every-one, including the lecturer. You need to select quiet and comfortable surroundings.

Lectures and demonstrations that take place in the stable yard must be planned with regard to safety, weather conditions and visibility. Crowding a group of students into a small stable with a horse is potentially dangerous, as the horse may kick out or swing round. Even if the horse behaves well, it is still unlikely that everyone will have a good view. However, if just one or two students are attending the lecture, the stable could be a suitable environment, providing the horse is tied up and everyone keeps to the same side of the horse at the same time.

Ideally, stable yard lectures should take place with the horse tied up outside, leaving enough room for the students to stand or sit round in a large semicircle. They should be well away from the horse so that there is no danger of kicks, etc. This will also give the lecturer room to move safely around the horse. If weather conditions are poor, this area needs to be under cover and well lit. All yard areas should be enclosed so that if the horse gets loose there will be gates and fences blocking all its exits.

2. Voice

Providing you know your subject well and have made a good plan, you should have no difficulty in knowing what to say. However, it is the way it is said that makes all the difference. Students need a clear and interesting voice to listen to. If you speak too slowly or too fast, with too many "umms", etc., you will not hold the students' attention. It can be helpful to make a tape recording of one of your lectures and listen to yourself. Each individual will have different problems to overcome. Think of pausing instead of saying "umm", vary the tone of your voice and try to speak with enthusiasm.

Reading directly from your notes will not work as you will be looking down all the time, unable to see the students' reactions. In this situation, the students might as well read a book on their own. Notes should be used to remind you of each point you intend to cover but the main content should be in your head. For this reason, you must know your subject thoroughly!

3. Visual Aids

The visual aid is very powerful and should help most people to understand and retain information. Your choice of what to use and when will affect the quality of the lecture.

Handouts

A clear photocopy for the student to keep and refer back to will eliminate the need for hasty sketches during the lecture or inaccurate drawings made from memory. Throughout this book there is a series of drawings that are designed to be used as "masters", from which copies can be made. It is better to issue such handouts at the end of a lecture, having already told the students that they will be available, otherwise they become a distraction, drawing attention away from the speaker.

Overhead Projector (OHP)

Providing you use this simple piece of equipment well, it will help you to convey information. You must set up the OHP in advance. Project a drawing onto the screen, then stand at the back of the room and make sure it is clearly visible. The whole procedure becomes an annoying distraction if the picture/printing is too small or blurred to be understood. Check that you are also expert at putting the acetate in the right way up!

   Although you have prepared handouts for the end of the lecture, you will probably need to draw the students' attention to particular items during the lecture. For example, in "Shoeing" you may not have real examples of all the tools available. If you draw and display them individually on the OHP, however, the students' attention will be focused on each item as you choose to show it.

   The OHP enlarges pictures, which is particularly advantageous when working with large groups of students. You can also build up pictures by laying one acetate on top of another.

   Making up the acetates in advance facilitates the flow of your lecture and saves time. The acetates can be kept and used over and over again.

Pictures/Photographs

When a particular item is not available to you, a picture of that item is the next best thing. It is a good idea to compile a folder of useful pictures; for example, different breeds or colours of horses, poisonous plants, types of rugs, etc. Taking photographs is a good way of adding to your collection, especially if you photograph interesting events that may not be a daily occurrence; for example, a mare foaling or a vet giving treatment. If you have photos made into slides, they are even more useful, providing you have a slide projector. The time taken to pass a picture around a large group will interrupt the flow of your lecture, therefore pictures are most useful for small groups who can gather around and look at the picture together.

Video

Combining both sight and sound, the video is an excellent way of putting information across. Always watch the video yourself first, to check its content and quality, before showing it to the students.

Blackboard and Chalk, or White Board and Pens

These are useful for those quick illustrations that help you to explain a particular point to a particular group, providing you are a confident illustrator and can spell properly!

Although you can prepare a little by writing headings or drawing on the blackboard before your lecture, it is not a permanent way of presenting your subject and can be time wasting in the long run.

Flip Chart

A useful aid that can be set up more easily than the OHP. Headings and illustrations can be drawn and reused many times.

Demonstrations

This is probably the most useful form of visual instruction for stable management and the only real, three-dimensional way of showing students how a job is done.

Props

Combining seeing and touching makes a lecture more interesting and easier to understand. For example, being able to handle the shoeing tools or a clipping machine, is far more effective than just looking at pictures. Props also help you to employ the senses of smell and taste. Aromas can be powerful memory jerkers and can help to focus the students' attention. This can be helpful when learning about feed stuffs and veterinary applications.

In order to make sure that the information you give has been absorbed and understood, you will need to obtain feedback from the students. While watching students carry out various tasks, and by asking them questions, you will soon discover whether or not they have understood and remembered everything they have been taught. At the end of each lecture I have given suggestions for follow-up work. During these sessions, you should obtain sufficient feedback to tell if you are being successful with your lecturing techniques.

You can also gain feedback during each lecture by listening to questions asked, looking at students' reactions and by asking questions yourself.

The students also need feedback from the lecturer. They need to know if they are interpreting instructions and answering questions correctly. They need to know if the standard of their work is acceptable. So feedback is very important in both directions.

By using different lecturing techniques you will accommodate the needs of a range of students who learn and absorb information in various ways. However, you should be careful not to let the use of resources become more important than the content of the lecture. It is possible to use too many visual aids and demonstrations, which can result in confusion. For this reason, most lectures should consist of a balanced combination of theory, demonstration and/or active partici-pation, along with a carefully selected variety of resources. For each of the following lectures you will need to select your resources according to availability and the size and type of group to which you are lecturing.

2 Points of the Horse and Identification

Time

1 hour 30 minutes

Resources

a. A horse that will stand quietly when tied up outside. (Have a mare, gelding and, if possible, a stallion.)
b. A selection of horses and ponies that have different colours and markings.
c. Handouts.
d. Pictures, showing other colours and markings that are not illustrated by the horses you have available.
e. Measuring stick.

Location

Stable yard; if possible, an enclosed, undercover area, with room for students to gather around the horse at a safe distance.

Preparation

a. Copy the correct number of handouts for the students attending.
b. Make a note of the horses with different colours and markings that you will be using in the lecture.
c. The pictures of colours and markings may be displayed on a lecture room wall or carried with you in a folder.

FOR LECTURING PURPOSES

tail

point of buttock

point of hip

dock

point of hock

hind quarters

hock

tendons

fetlock

croup

thigh

loins

stifle

flank

gaskin or second thigh

back

sheath

cannon or shannon

withers

chestnut

pastern

coronet band

neck

hoof

crest

mane

poll

ears

forelock

forehead

projecting cheek bone

chin groove

nostril

cheek

throat

muzzle

jugular groove

wind pipe

point of shoulder

shoulder

breast or chest

forearm

knee

point of elbow

tendons

ergot

cannon

fetlock

bulbs of heel

pastern

coronet band

hoof

The points of the horse

d. Put the measuring stick within easy reach of the horse to be used.

e. Tie up the horse in a safe area.

Aim

- To teach the students the points of the horse and its different colours and markings.

Objective

- To show the students how to identify and describe horses and ponies.

1. Describing a Horse

With the horse tied up in the yard, work logically through all the points of the horse. Pause to let the students come forward to repeat and indicate these points.   (15 minutes)

2. Equine Gender

Using a mare, gelding and, where possible, a stallion, make sure the students can identify the different sexes. Explain the terminology used:

- Filly — This term is usually applied to a female horse until she is fully grown.
- Mare — A fully grown female horse.
- Colt — This term is usually applied to a male horse until he is fully grown or gelded.
- Stallion — A fully grown male horse that has not been gelded (i.e. "entire").
- Gelding — A male horse that has been castrated (the testes are removed) so that it cannot reproduce. Most male horses are gelded as this makes them easier to handle.
- Rig — This is a male horse with either one or both testes retained in the abdomen.   (10 minutes)

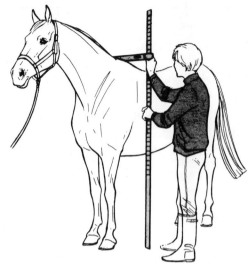

Measuring the horse's height

3. Height

Horses are measured in hands. One hand equals 4 in (approx. 10 cm). The height is always expressed in hands and inches; for example, 15.2 h.h. (The h.h. stands for "hands high".) The measurement is taken from the ground to the highest point of the horse's withers. For accurate measurement the horse should be asked to stand square, unshod, on level ground. If students know their own height in hands, it can help them to estimate the height of a horse. As the horse may be suspicious of the measuring stick, it should be untied before the students practise measuring.   (10 minutes)

4. Markings

Using the horses you have selected, show the students the following markings:

- White or striped hooves − These are usually accompanied by white leg markings.
- White socks − Front or hind limbs that are white from the coronet upwards, with any variation in height as far as the

knee or hock.
- White stockings — The same as white socks but describing any variation in height over and above the knee and hock.
- White coronet — If the white marking is so small that it hardly extends beyond the coronet, it would be misleading to call it a sock. In this situation it is called a white coronet.
- Ermine marks — These are black dots on a white sock. They usually only appear around the coronet and pastern.
- Star — A white mark in the middle of the forehead. It may be very small. If it covers a very wide area, it would be called a white forehead.
- Blaze — A large white patch on the forehead, extending down the middle of the face as a broad stripe, usually finishing at or near the end of the upper lip.
- Stripe — A white line, too narrow to be called a blaze but extending down the face in the same way.
- White nostril/lip, etc. — The best way to describe a small white marking anywhere around the muzzle. Also called a "snip".
- White face — Sometimes a blaze extends over such a wide area that it is better described in this way.
- White markings are often found in other areas, as a result of scarring. They are common around the withers, from old saddle sores. These should simply be described according to what you see. For example: "two small white marks on the near side of the withers".
- Black points — Horses with black stockings, a black mane and tail, black tips to the ears and a black muzzle are said to have black points.
- Dorsal or eel stripe — This is a long black stripe on the back, which extends from the withers along the line of the spine to the top of the tail. This is common in the dun-coloured horse.
- Mealy muzzle — This is a light, biscuit-brown colouring covering the muzzle.
- Flaxen mane and tail — Some horses (mostly chestnuts) have manes and tails of a creamy-yellow colour, termed flaxen.
- Whorls — These are areas where hair grows out in different directions from one point. They are individual to each horse,

J.A.Allen & Co.Ltd.
The Horseman's Publisher

star

stripe

white face

blaze

snip

white sock

white stocking

white coronet

ermine marks

Face and leg markings

just as fingerprints are individual to humans. Whorls are often rosette-shaped. Those that extend upwards/sideways are termed feathered.

- Dapples − These look like a series of circles incorporated into the horse's colouring. Most common in the dapple grey, but many bays are also dappled.   (20 minutes)

5. Colours

Using the horses you have selected, show the students the following colours:

- Bay − The body colouring of the horse is brown. The mane and tail must be black. The bay may have socks or stockings and various face markings. They often have black points and may have a mealy muzzle. There are many different shades of bay: mahogany bay, bright bay, dark bay, light bay. Bays have dark skin and are the most likely colour to have ermine marks.
- Chestnut − A yellow/ginger/brown colour, varying from light to dark, with mane and tail a similar colouring to the body or flaxen. (The mane and tail cannot be black, as the horse would then be a bay.) Chestnuts can have any combination of socks, stockings and face markings. Many chestnuts have pale, sensitive skin. A darker brown, without the yellow tint, is called a liver chestnut.
- Grey − Generally quite dark in colouring as youngsters, greys gradually turn whiter. Their skin is dark and the coat contains a mixture of black, grey and white hairs. Very dark greys are called iron grey, those with circle-like patterns in their coats are called dapple grey, and those with a freckled appearance are called flea bitten grey.
- Roan − A dark-skinned horse with white hairs mixed evenly into the main coat colouring. The black mane and tail also contain a mixture of white hairs. Shades of roan: strawberry, blue, grey, bay, red.
- Piebald − The coat consists of patches of black hair and patches of white. The pattern of these patches will vary tremendously.

The mane and tail will usually be coloured according to the colour of the coat at their base of growth. For example, if the horse has black hair partway down its neck and then white hair, the mane will, correspondingly, be black partway and then white. The horse's skin will be dark under the black hair and pink under the white hair.

- Skewbald — As for piebald, but with brown and white or any other colour patches. Both skewbald and piebald are often referred to as "coloured" horses.
- Black — The coat, mane and tail must definitely be black, with no traces of brown hair. Any combination of white leg and face markings is acceptable.
- Dun — The skin is dark but the main body of the coat is a pale biscuit-coloured brown. Duns have black points and a dorsal stripe. As with all colourings, there are different shades. If the coat is more creamy than brown in colour, it is called yellow dun.
- Cream — The skin is pale and the coat, mane and tail are all a creamy-white colour. It is sometimes possible to distinguish white leg and face markings on this cream coat.
- Brown — The skin is dark and the coat, mane and tail are evenly dark brown. A brown horse is similar to a bay but does not have black points.
- Appaloosa — A dark-skinned horse with a spotted coat. The coat is usually predominantly grey, with brown or black spots. There is an Appaloosa Society which lays down strict rules as to colouring.
- Palomino — This colouring is like a very pale chestnut, but not as pale as a cream, with a flaxen mane and tail. The Palomino Society lays down very specific regulations as to permitted colouring.   (20 minutes)

6. Description

Finally, put all this information together and describe a horse. For example, a 14.2 h.h. bay gelding. Black points, except for a white sock on the near hind. White star and white stripe tapering towards the nearside nostril, etc.   (10 minutes)

Further Points

1. Colours and markings are used as identification details on registration papers and vaccination cards. As no two horses have the same combination of whorls, they are of particular importance for identification.
2. Freeze branding is another way of marking and identifying horses. Branding irons are cooled in liquid nitrogen. When applied to the skin, they destroy the pigment cells so that white hair grows through, leaving a permanent mark.
3. Hot-iron branding is also used. Applied to the skin, it is mostly used for native ponies and some traditional breeds from abroad, such as the Hanoverian. A new form of hot-iron branding, painless to the horse, involves branding the owner's post code onto the horse's hooves. Owners have branding irons made up and their farriers apply them. As the marks grow out, they are reapplied, approximately every six months. (5 minutes)

Follow-up Work

1. The students should practise describing many different types of horse and demonstrate their ability to measure accurately.
2. To confirm their knowledge of the points of the horse, ask the students to show you each point in turn.
3. Question and answer:
    a. Why are whorls so important in the identification of horses?
    b. What is freeze branding?
    c. Explain the hot-iron branding system that is used on horses' hooves.

3   Handling Horses in Everyday Situations

Time

1 hour 40 minutes

Resources

a. An easy-to-catch horse in the field.
b. A horse in a stable.
c. Head collars and ropes.
d. A bridle.
e. Hard hat, gloves and whip.
f. Handouts.

Location

a. The lecture room.
b. The field.
c. The stable yard.

Preparation

a. Copy the correct number of handouts for the students attending.
b. Check that you have head collars and bridles to fit the horses you intend to use.
c. Have your hat, gloves and whip available.

Aim

- To teach the students the basic methods of handling horses in fields and stables.

Objectives

- To make students aware of safety when handling horses.
- To increase the students' awareness of the horse's instincts and behavioural patterns.

1. Catching a Horse from the Field

Starting in the lecture room, explain the procedure to be followed when catching a horse from the field.

a. If the horse is likely to be difficult to catch, take a reward, like a carrot or some pony cubes, in your pocket. If there are several horses in the field, they may gather around you expecting feed. You could find yourself caught in the middle of biting and kicking as these horses chase each other away. This is why it is not advisable to take a bucket into the field, as it will immediately attract the attention of all the horses.

b. Make sure you have a suitably sized head collar with a strong rope, and wear gloves to protect your hands while leading. If the horse is young or apt to be difficult, also wear a hard hat.

c. Enter the field and close the gate securely behind you.

d. Approach the horse quietly, walking towards its shoulder, with the head collar concealed behind your back if the horse is likely to be difficult. Remember that the horse has a blind spot immediately behind and in front of it. If you approach in this blind spot, you will startle it. If the horse does not appear to have seen you, announce your approach by calling its name. This may also encourage the horse to come towards you, which is preferable to you walking a long way into the field. There is less chance of having problems with other horses or the horse you are leading if you are only a short distance from the gate.

Leading in hand

e. Allow the horse to smell you. Stroke its neck, then slip the rope over its neck to secure an initial hold on it.

f. Standing close into its neck, facing forward, put on the head collar. In this way the horse can see what you are doing and you can move back with the horse if it steps backwards. If you stand in front of the horse, in its blind spot, it may move away and you will lose your hold on it.

g. Lead it in, keeping by its shoulder, encouraging it to walk on beside you and not to lag behind. Don't restrict the horse's head but hold the rope close to the head collar to give maximum control if needed. Never wrap a rope around your hand. If the horse pulls, the rope will tighten and you are likely to be trapped and injured.

h. Most gates open into the field to help to prevent horses from barging out. You can teach your horse to step back as you open the gate.

i. Always give the horse plenty of room in the gateway. If it hits its side, it will soon start to rush through gateways in the fear of being hurt.
j. Close the gate securely behind you.   (15 minutes)

2. Practice

Now take the students out to the field and catch the horse, following this procedure. If the horse is close enough for the students to observe you from the gate, they should watch from outside the field.

(10 minutes)

3. Tying Up

Demonstrate the correct method of tying up.

a. It is advisable to tie horses to a piece of string, rather than directly to a metal ring. The string should not break too easily but if the horse pulls hard in panic, it should give way. Once the horse has broken free it will probably soon relax. (It is important to have an enclosed yard, to prevent a loose horse from escaping.) If the horse cannot break free of the rope, it will go on panicking and may even throw itself to the ground.
b. Tie up using a slip knot. You should always be able to release a horse quickly. Allow the horse enough rope to have free movement of its head, but not so much that it may get a leg caught over the rope. You may wish to tie the horse on a very short rope while grooming, especially if it is inclined to nip.   (10 minutes)

4. Handling

Show the students how to handle the horse while working around it.

a. When approaching a tied-up horse, go quietly towards its shoulder, using the horse's name. As you move around the horse, to groom, tack up, etc., keep in contact with it by running a hand over its coat. In this way it will remain

J.A. Allen & Co. Ltd.
The Horseman's Publisher

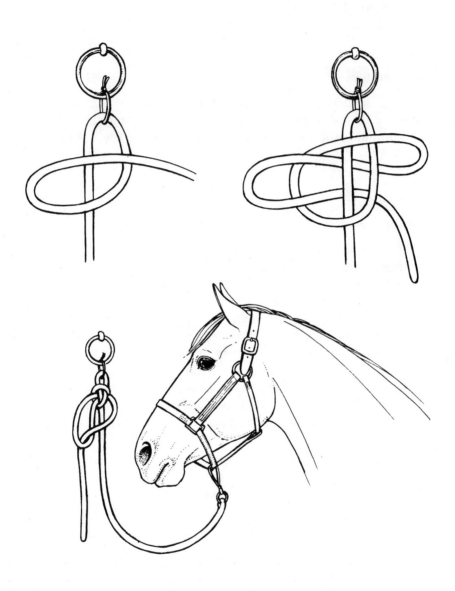

Tie up using a slip knot

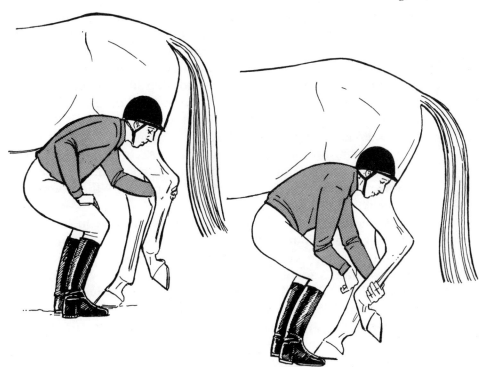

The correct technique for picking up a hind foot, avoiding wrapping your arm around the hind leg

constantly aware of your presence. Unexpected movements will trigger the flight or fight instincts of the horse. It may, for example, pull back or kick out.

b. When grooming down the legs or putting on boots, never kneel down. Just squat down, so that you can move away quickly. Pick up a hind leg by running your hand down the front of the limb. Do *not* wrap your arm around the back of the limb, as you may get caught up if the horse kicks out.

c. The horse should be taught to move over on command. Place your hand on its flank or hind quarters and apply firm pressure, at the same time saying "Over". Repeat until you get the desired reaction. Praise the horse each time and it will soon move over willingly as soon as you give the command.

d. As it can be difficult to apply boots and bandages while the horse is resting a leg, it is also necessary to teach the horse to stand with its weight on all four feet when required. Using the "Over" command will often achieve this aim. Alternatively, you may need to ask the horse to step back. Stand in front and a little to one side of it. Place one hand on the head collar and one hand in the middle of the horse's chest with your thumb at the base of its neck, and the rest of your hand pushing against it, at the same time saying "Back". Repeat the command until you get the desired result. Praise the horse, and it will soon learn to respond to the command "Back".

e. Take note of how your horse reacts to you as you handle it. For example, it may threaten to bite you when you use a dandy brush on certain parts of its body. Don't just tell it off, as constant repetition of this problem is likely to make it resentful so that it bites and kicks more aggressively. Instead, you should look for a solution to the problem. Perhaps use a different brush or use the brush more gently or even more firmly, so that you do not irritate or tickle the horse in the first place.   (15 minutes)

5. Approaching a Horse

Show the students how to approach a horse in the stable.

a. Always encourage the stabled horse to come to the door before you go into the stable. In this way you can go in, slip on the head collar and be in control of the situation.

b. If the horse will not come to the door, and especially if it turns its quarters towards you, encourage it with a handful of feed until it has learnt the habit of greeting you at the door. It should, however, step back immediately if you give the command "Back", to avoid the possibility of it barging out as you open the door.

c. Once in the stable with the head collar on, you can tie the horse up and adjust rugs, groom, muck out, etc. Remember to approach the tied-up horse as described above. Whatever part of the horse you need to approach, for example, a hind leg to put on a boot, always go to the shoulder first, then run your hand over the horse's coat to that area. Never just "dive in", as the horse may not be aware of your intentions. (10 minutes)

6. Leading

Demonstrate how to lead a horse out of the stable and stand it in the yard for veterinary or other inspection.

a. In order to have full control of the horse, especially as a vet may cause it to become agitated, it should be lead out in a bridle. The handler should wear gloves and a hard hat.

b. Take care to lead the horse straight through the centre of the doorway. Do not try to turn the horse until it is clear, as the horse's hips are particularly vulnerable if knocked against the side. If the horse is hurt in this way, it will begin rushing through doorways, which will exacerbate the likelihood of injury.

c. For inspection by the vet, potential purchaser, etc., the horse should be asked to stand with its weight supported squarely on all four feet. To achieve this, lead the horse in an active walk on a straight line. Steady the horse, then give the command "and stand". If it hasn't halted squarely, you can encourage each leg into position by asking the horse to step back or take another step forward, as necessary.

d. Stand in front of the horse, facing it and a little to one side. Take one rein in each hand to give you control. By not standing directly in front, you avoid being kicked by the horse if it strikes out with a forelimb.

e. As the person looking at the horse moves around it, from one side to the other, so the handler should move in order to be on the same side of the horse as that person. This also applies to the horse in the stable or tied up on the yard, etc. The idea is to minimise the risk of one person being kicked, stepped on or crushed by the horse swinging sideways or lashing out. For example, two people on the same side of the horse can move its quarters away from them by turning its head towards them. (15 minutes)

7. Leading in Walk and Trot

Demonstrate how to lead a horse in hand at walk and trot.

a. The horse should be in a bridle, in order to give the handler control.

b. The handler should wear gloves and a hard hat and carry a stick.

c. Walk by the horse's nearside shoulder and look straight ahead. Do not move ahead of the horse nor turn to look at it. This will discourage the horse, making it more likely to resist.

d. Use your voice to say "Walk on" or "Trot", and encourage the horse, if necessary, by using the stick in your left hand. Reach behind you and flick the horse's side or quarters.

e. One hand should hold the reins close to the bit, without restricting the horse's head. The other hand should hold the end of the reins so that they do not trail on the ground nor get caught round your feet!

f. The horse is generally led from the near side but it is useful for it to learn to be led from both sides.

g. By walking the horse positively on a straight line and not interfering with its head movement, observers will be able to see how the horse moves.

h. When you turn the horse, turn it away from you. In this way you will maintain better control and balance. If you swing the horse around you, it can easily pull back and get away from you or step on you.

i. The same procedure applies to leading the horse in trot. Make sure, however, that the horse has returned to walk before you start to turn it and that it is completely straight after the turn before you ask it to trot again. Horses have been made to slip and fall by handlers rushing into trot after a turn or not taking time to steady the horse before turning.

j. When you return the horse to the stable, turn it around to face the doorway and check that the door is closed, before you remove the head collar or bridle. In this way you can slip out of the stable and will not risk being trapped in the corner of the box by a horse that has turned its hind legs towards you.   (15 minutes)

8. Turning Out

Now demonstrate how to turn the horse out into the field.

    a. Wearing gloves and possibly a hard hat, lead your horse out to the field in a head collar and rope.

    b. Keep hold of the gate as you lead the horse in, to minimise the risk of other horses escaping. Close the gate securely behind you.

    c. Turn the horse to face the gate before you let it go. This will give you time to move away from the horse before it turns and moves off. Some horses rush off and kick out at the same time, so if you haven't had time to move away you could get kicked. You could offer the horse a titbit to discourage it from rushing off.

    d. If several horses are being turned out, let them all go at the same time. This prevents a horse trying to pull away in its desire to follow another one that has been let loose.

    e. Having let the horses go, don't chase them into the field. This will only encourage the horses to pull away and kick out.

    f. Finally, no matter how well you know your horse, it is never worth taking risks with your safety. Horses are unpredictable, and those with the quietest natures can sometimes behave badly. By handling all horses correctly and making sure that they respond in the right way, you will establish a good relationship with each horse. This should produce well-behaved horses and minimise the likelihood of accidents.

(10 minutes)

Follow-up Work

1. The students should be observed and corrected in their daily handling of the horses they work with. Constant correction will help to make safe handling procedures become automatic.

2. As a project, more experienced students could be allocated a young horse to teach it good manners through correct handling.

3. Question and answer sessions will help to confirm the students'
   knowledge:

   a. Should you take feed into the field when catching horses?
   b. What equipment do you need when leading horses out for
      veterinary inspection?
   c. How should you approach a horse in the field, and why?
   d. How would you ask your horse to move over or step back in
      the stable?
   e. Why is it so important to lead a horse straight through door-
      ways and gateways?
   f. Why is it advisable to tie horses to a piece of string, rather
      than directly to the tying-up ring?
   g. Is it advisable to kneel down beside a horse?
   h. When going into a stable, why should you encourage the
      horse to come to the door first?
   i. When you are holding a horse for inspection, why should you
      keep to the same side of the horse as the person inspecting it?
   j. Explain the procedure for turning horses out in fields.

4 Strapping/Grooming/ Quartering

Time

1 hour 20 minutes

Resources

a. A horse or pony that will tolerate all types of grooming tools and stand quietly (preferably outside) for the duration of the lecture.
b. A complete set of grooming tools, including different types of each item.
c. Grooming machine. (An extension cable may be necessary.)
d. Two buckets or bowls of water.
e. Handouts.

Location

Stable yard. An enclosed area, if possible, for safety reasons. Allow room for students to gather around at a safe distance. Under cover would be ideal; for example, an indoor school.

NB It would not be suitable to give the lecture with students inside a stable, as they will not be able to move clear if the horse fidgets.

Preparation

a. Copy the correct number of handouts for the students attending.
b. Lay out grooming tools/machine and water buckets within easy reach of the horse.
c. Tie up horse/pony in selected area.

Aim

- To teach the students the most safe and effective method of strapping/grooming/quartering.

Objectives

- To clean the horse thoroughly, which will also stimulate circulation and promote health.
- To improve the appearance of the horse.
- To aid the prevention of disease.
- To build a relationship with the horse.

1. The Grooming Kit

Identify each item of grooming kit, explaining, and briefly demonstrating, its use.

- Hoof pick — For removing packed-in dirt and stones from the hoof. Used from the heel towards the toe to prevent the point of the hoof pick accidentally digging into the frog or heels.
- Dandy brush — For removing dry mud from the coat. Usually only used on the legs and on unclipped, less-sensitive parts of the body. The dandy brush should not be used on the mane or tail, as it will break the hairs. Use in short firm strokes.
- Body brush — For removing grease and dust from the coat. Generally used on stable-kept horses, all over the body, including the mane and tail. Used more sparingly on the grass-kept horse as it needs the grease in its coat to protect it from the weather. Being soft, it is the best brush to use on the horse's face and any other sensitive areas. It is used in conjunction with the metal curry comb. When using the body brush on the near side of the horse, hold it in your left hand, and in your right hand when on the off side. This enables you to put more strength into the slightly semicircular movement with which the brush should be firmly applied.

J.A. Allen & Co. Ltd.
The Horseman's Publisher

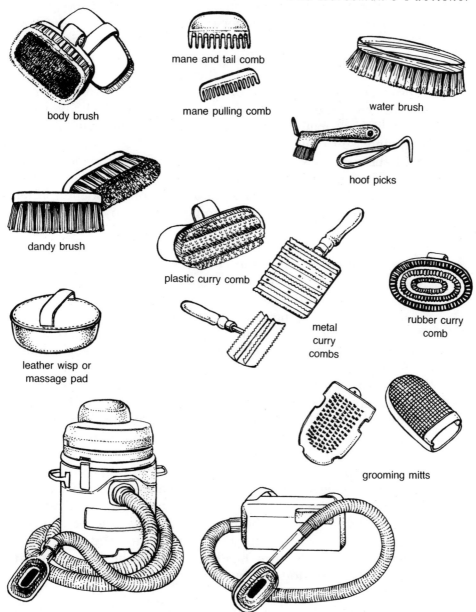

body brush

mane and tail comb

mane pulling comb

water brush

hoof picks

dandy brush

plastic curry comb

metal curry combs

rubber curry comb

leather wisp or massage pad

grooming mitts

electric grooming machines

Grooming tools

- Metal curry comb — For removing grease from the body bush. It is *never* used on the horse. After each stroke, the body brush should be drawn across the curry comb, which is held in the opposite hand. The grease is then knocked from the curry comb by tapping it on the ground.
- Rubber curry comb — For removing grease from the coat. Normally used on stable-kept horses, all over the body. Firmly applied in small circles, against the lie of the hair, it brings the grease to the surface.
- Plastic curry comb — For removing mud and the loose winter coat during moulting. It is generally used on grass-kept horses, all over the body. It should not be used on the mane and tail, as it will break the hairs. It can be used in any kind of stroke necessary to remove the mud and loose coat. Also used to clean the body brush, it makes a good and safe substitute for the metal curry comb, especially for children.
- Mane comb — For removing tangles from the mane. It may also be used on the tail. It is used in a simple combing action, taking a small portion of hair at a time.
- Stable rubber — For removing dust from the surface of the horse's coat after grooming. It can be used all over the horse, just like a duster.
- Wisp/massage pad — For improving muscle tone. It can be used on muscular areas, mainly on the topline of the horse, for example on the trapezius muscle of the neck and the muscles of the hind quarters. It is used in conjunction with a stable rubber. The horse should be able to see the wisp being raised, so that it can tense its muscles in preparation as the wisp is "banged" down. The muscle area is then relaxed by a stroke with the stable rubber. These two actions are repeated in a rhythm, causing the horse alternately to tense and relax the muscles, which helps to tone them up. The wisp should not be used violently. The "bang" should be firm enough to cause the horse to tense but not so hard that it causes pain or fear.
- Grooming mit — For removing grease and dust from the horse's coat. It can be used on any part of the horse's body, including the head. A mit is generally made of cactus cloth or

rubber. Both types are stroked firmly over the body. The rubber type will lift grease to the surface, while the cactus cloth type will lift off surface grease/dust and help to create a shine on the coat.

- Cactus cloth — Has the same use as the grooming mit described above, but is in the form of a duster-sized cloth.
- Water brush — For applying water to the coat/mane/tail, in order to lay the hair or to wash it. It can be used on any part of the horse, including the feet.
- Sponges — For washing the horse's eyes, nostrils and under the dock. You should have separate sponges, one for each area.   (20 minutes)

2. Strapping/Grooming/Quartering

The process of strapping/grooming/quartering should follow a logical pattern. For example, there is little point in grooming the neck before the mane, as dirt from the mane would then fall on the neck, which would then need to be groomed again. Obviously this would be a time-wasting exercise. Describe each process and demonstrate where necessary.

Strapping

The full grooming process, including wisping. Generally used for the fit, stable-kept horse, it will take half to three-quarters of an hour to complete.

Method
a. Use a hoof pick to pick out the feet. Check the condition of the feet and shoes at the same time.
b. Remove mud from the coat with the dandy brush.
c. Groom the mane and forelock with the body brush and/or mane comb.
d. Groom the head with the body brush.
e. Bring all the grease to the surface with the rubber curry comb and/or the rubber grooming mit.

   f. Use the body brush and metal curry comb together to remove all the grease and dust.

   g. Groom the tail with the body brush and your fingers.

   h. Wisp if required.

   i. Wash the eyes and nostrils, and under the dock, with two separate sponges and warm water.

   j. Lay the mane and tail with the water brush.

   k. Put a final shine on the coat by dusting over with the stable rubber and/or the cactus cloth/mit.

Grooming

Basic cleaning of the horse. Generally used to prepare the grass-kept horse/pony for work, it will take 15–30 minutes to complete. "Grooming" is the word most commonly used to describe any brushing/cleaning of the horse.

Method

   a. Pick out the feet.

   b. Remove mud and loose coat with the dandy brush and plastic curry comb.

   c. Groom the mane and forelock with the body brush and/or mane comb.

   d. Groom the head with the body brush.

   e. Groom the tail with the body brush and your fingers.

   f. In the summer, remove excess grease and dust by lightly body brushing all over. Do not remove too much grease as it is essential for waterproofing and protection, especially in the winter.

   g. Finally, wash the eyes, nostrils and under the dock.

Quartering

Basic cleaning of the rugged, stable-kept horse prior to work, by folding back the rug in four successive quarters. Designed as a quick tidy-up session before riding, it should only take 10–15 minutes.

Method

a. Pick out feet.
b. Remove stable stains from the legs with the dandy brush.
c. Groom the head with the body brush.
d. Tidy up the mane and remove any bedding with the body brush.
e. Undo the breast and belly straps of the rug. Folding back a quarter of the rug at a time, remove stable stains, etc., with the body brush.
f. Use the water brush and warm water for any heavy stains that will not brush out.
g. Tidy up the tail and remove any bedding with the body brush, and your fingers.
h. Finally, sponge the eyes, nostrils and under the dock.

(25 minutes)

Further Points

1. Always tie your horse up before grooming. You risk being cornered in the stable and may be kicked or bitten, especially if you are grooming a sensitive spot.
2. All the brushes can be used in a to and fro action, against the lie of the hair, to help remove mud, grease, etc. However, you should always finish with a stroke that lays the hair flat in its direction of growth.
3. Brushes will not remove grease and mud from a wet coat, so leave a wet horse to dry before grooming.
4. When grooming the head, first untie the horse. Stand facing the horse. With one hand holding the head collar, use the other hand to body brush the front of the face. Start in the middle of the forehead and work upwards and outwards, and then down to the end of the nose. Then slip the head collar back around the horse's neck. To groom the near side of the face, stand with your right shoulder under the horse's throat, put your right arm around the off side of its face and place your hand on its nose. Your left hand is then free to brush the face. Repeat on the other side. Then replace the head collar and tie up.

5. The head collar should never be put around the horse's neck while it is tied up. If the horse steps back or is startled, the head collar may tighten around its throat or slip over its head. The horse may then panic and break loose.

6. To groom the mane, brush all of it over onto the opposite side to that on which it normally lies. With the body brush or mane comb, bring a few hairs at a time towards you, and brush thoroughly to remove dirt and tangles. Start at the poll and work towards the withers, until you have groomed the whole mane.

7. To groom the tail, stand to the side of the horse, never directly behind it. Stand close in to the horse's quarters and take the whole tail in one hand. With the other hand, use the body brush to brush down a few hairs at a time. Difficult tangles can be loosened with your fingers. You can work through the whole tail with your fingers if you prefer.

8. If your horse is quite tall, stand on a stool or box to make sure you get all of it really clean.

9. While grooming, constantly run your spare hand over the horse. In this way you will feel dirt, scabs, lumps, heat, etc., that may be forming, for example, under the hair or under the belly, that are not visible. This is especially important when grooming the legs. You should constantly compare the two forelegs and the two hind legs, as this will help you to detect abnormalities at the earliest possible stage.

10. Use your grooming time to learn about every inch of your horse.

11. Always put loose hair, and pick out feet, into a skip to keep the yard area tidy.

12. Wash the whole grooming kit regularly. If you are using it every day, it will probably need to be washed once a week.

(20 minutes)

The Grooming Machine

Although not found in every yard, this can be an excellent labour-saving device. There are many types, for example, hand held or strapped to the waist. As with any electrical equipment, safety is very important.

First check that the plug and lead are secure and that no wires are exposed. Once plugged in, make sure the lead cannot be trodden on by the horse. Suspend it from a hook or over a door. Some horses may be worried about the machine at first. However, if you introduce it carefully, most horses will soon settle. It will also help to accustom some horses to clipping machines if they have not been clipped before. A grooming machine works like a small vacuum cleaner, drawing the dust and grease out of the horse's coat and cleaning very thoroughly with little effort required from the groom. It is sometimes thought, however, that the horse misses out on the massaging effect created by manual grooming.

Demonstrate your particular grooming machine to the students.

(15 minutes)

Follow-up Work

1. The students should be watched and corrected where necessary while strapping, grooming and quartering their horses. With practice, they will become efficient at grooming both manually and with the machine.
2. Question and answer sessions will help to confirm their knowledge:
    a. Why is it necessary to groom horses?
    b. What is each of the brushes used for?
    c. What is wisping?
    d. What is meant by quartering?
    e. Why is it important to use your hands as a grooming tool?

5   Bedding and the Mucking Out Procedure

Time

1 hour 20 minutes

Resources

a. Two stables that require mucking out. One with straw bedding and the other with shavings.
b. A complete set of mucking out tools.
c. A quiet horse.
d. Handouts.
e. Clean bedding for topping up.
f. Samples of different types of bedding: wheat/barley/oat straw, shavings, paper.

Location

Lecture room, then the stable yard.

Preparation

a. Copy handouts for the students attending.
b. Arrange the mucking out tools, preferably under cover, a safe distance from where the horse will be tied.
c. Put the clean bedding in an accessible area, under cover, out of reach of the horse.
d. Tie up the horse in the selected area.
e. Lay out bedding samples in the lecture room.

Aims

- To teach the students how to muck out stables and handle different tools and bedding.

Objectives

- To keep the stables clean, thereby helping to prevent disease.
- To make students aware of economy in their disposal of the bedding.
- To improve understanding of the horse's comfort and needs.

Starting in the lecture room, run through the theory (using the bedding samples) to prepare the students for the practical work to follow.

1. Bedding Systems

- Complete mucking out − All the soiled bedding is removed every day and the floor swept clean, therefore all the bedding is moved. It would take an experienced person 15−20 minutes to muck out an average-sized stable.
- Deep litter − With minimum disturbance of the bedding, all the droppings and very wet patches are removed. The remaining bedding is levelled out and clean bedding is placed on top. This is a less time-consuming process than complete mucking out, taking only 10−15 minutes. A deep base of dry, rotting bedding gradually builds up. This base provides warmth and protection. However, it would not be practical to allow the base to become deeper than approximately 20−25 cm (8−10 in). Therefore, the entire bed will need to be removed every three or four weeks. This is hard, time-consuming work if done manually. Stables designed with tractor access make the process much easier.
- Combined system − It may suit your life style to deep litter your stable during the week and completely muck it out at the weekend.

2. Types of Bedding

- Straw — Probably the most commonly used bedding, as it is relatively inexpensive and fairly easy to dispose of. There are three types of straw:
  i. Wheat — which is best, being the most resilient.
  ii. Barley — which is a little less tough.
  iii. Oat — which is not as suitable as it is soft and very palatable.
  A good sample of straw should be clean, free from mould and be strong-stemmed, thus allowing moisture to drain through the bed, leaving the horse with dry standing on top.
- Shavings — A popular bedding for horses that are inclined to eat straw and also for those that have respiratory allergies. It is more expensive than straw and difficult to dispose of if you are using large amounts. A shavings bed is more absorbent than a straw one and must be well handled to prevent it from becoming soggy. A good bale should contain large clean shavings, a minimum of dust and no debris, such as pieces of wood, etc. If purchased in plastic-wrapped bales, shavings can be stored outside. This is a great advantage if barn space is limited.
- Paper — A dust-free, inedible bedding, particularly suited to horses with respiratory problems. It comes in the form of diced or shredded newspaper. However, most people find it hard to work with. Being very absorbent, it can become packed down and difficult to remove unless the bed is frequently "fluffed up", as it does not have the "spring back" quality of straw and shavings. If purchased in plastic-wrapped bales, it can also be stored outside.
- Rubber — Now popular in horse boxes and trailers, where it has taken over from conventional bedding, but not yet a very popular form of flooring for stables. It is considered more hygienic, more slip-resistant, warmer and harder wearing than conventional flooring. In the stable it can be labour saving and eliminates the daily/weekly/monthly problem of bedding disposal. Many owners feel that rubber on its own doesn't provide necessary warmth and comfort, while others argue

that horses lie down happily in the field and don't need the comfort of soft bedding. In trials, some horses appear to feel the cold more, some lie down as often as before, and others less so.

Used without bedding, the rubber flooring can be washed down each day. Droppings need to be removed frequently to prevent the horse from getting very dirty when lying down.

Rubber can be used with conventional bedding but, being a softer than normal flooring, it only requires a thin layer of straw, shavings, etc.

3. Full Mucking Out Procedure for a Straw Bed

a. Assemble the tools:
- Four-prong fork
- Broom
- Shovel
- Wheelbarrow

b. Remove the horse from the stable, or tie up securely in the stable.

c. Hook back the door and place the wheelbarrow sideways on across the doorway. Set this way there are fewer sharp edges protruding into the stable.

d. Remove the obvious piles of droppings with the fork, by lifting the straw under the droppings, and then tip the droppings into the wheelbarrow. The straw can then be replaced in the bed.

e. Next choose one wall against which to put all the clean bedding. Work around the stable, tossing all the clean straw into a pile against this wall and placing all the soiled straw and droppings in the wheelbarrow.

f. Use the broom to sweep the floor clean and then shovel up the remaining debris.

g. Now put the straw back down as a bed.

h. Top up with fresh bedding.

i. Empty the wheelbarrow and put away the tools.

j. Untie the horse and check that it is securely bolted into its stable.

4. Variations for Full Mucking Out of a Shavings Bed

a. Wearing rubber gloves, remove the obvious droppings by hand, placing them straight into a skip. If you prefer, this can be done with a shavings fork.

b. Work through the whole bed with a shavings fork, removing the soiled patches and putting the clean bedding to one side.

(30 minutes)

5. Practical Demonstration

Move to the stable yard and give the students a practical demonstration, following points (a)–(j) on page 39. Initially without the horse in the stable, and then with it in the stable, demonstrate mucking out and relaying a straw/shavings bed, stressing the following points:

a. The door of the stable must always be securely hooked back. If left swinging, it could hit a passing horse or person, frighten a horse or be broken. Always secure doors.

b. Throw away as little bedding as possible. It is expensive and cost should always be considered. Disposal of bedding can be difficult, so don't add to the problem unnecessarily.

c. Choose a different wall to pile the clean straw against each day. In this way no part of the floor goes unswept for longer than a day or two at a time.

d. Keep sweeping to a minimum by loading your wheelbarrow correctly. As you muck out, fill the four corners of your wheelbarrow first. This creates a dip in the middle into which the last shovelful of droppings can be placed. In this way you will not leave a trail behind you as you take your wheelbarrow to the muck heap.

e. If the horse is in the stable while you muck out, safety should be your first thought. The stable tools have the potential to injure the horse and the horse could then injure you. The horse *must* be tied up. However well behaved it is, it may be startled by external influences. This could lead to it barging into you and the tools or perhaps trying to jump out over the wheelbarrow − a potentially disastrous situation!

f. While working around the horse, make sure you keep the

J.A.Allen & Co.Ltd.
The Horseman's Publisher

Long or short handled four-pronged fork

shovel

yard brooms

wheelbarrow

shavings fork

skip and rake for droppings

Mucking out tools

tools, especially the fork, well away from it. Move the horse over to stand on the opposite side of the box to the one at which you are working.

g. If the horse is going out of its stable to work or to be turned out, the bed could be left up to allow the floor to dry or be disinfected.

h. If the horse is staying in its stable, the bed should be put down. Lay the remaining bedding evenly over the floor, then top up with approximately half a bale of fresh straw/shavings. Build banks around the edges to prevent injuries or the horse getting cast and to minimise draughts. The bed should be thick enough to protect the horse from the concrete floor. If the flooring is easily exposed when the horse moves around, the bed is too thin. Overly thick beds are wasteful and time consuming.

i. Some owners prefer to use a "day bed" and "night bed". After mucking out some of the bedding is laid, to make a slightly thinner bed that can be easily skipped out during the day. In the evening the rest of the bed is laid and fresh bedding is added, to make a thick night bed.

j. If the bed is skipped out frequently throughout the day, and again at evening stables, the job of mucking out the next morning is much easier.   (30 minutes)

6. Building and Maintaining the Muck Heap

At the muck heap, explain and demonstrate the following:

a. If the muck heap is well packed down it will rot more quickly. As it rots it will reduce in size. This helps to keep the muck heap at a manageable size.

b. Rotting muck heaps become very hot and can self-ignite, therefore it is essential to position the muck heap at a safe distance from buildings, although at the same time it should be easily accessible for workers with wheelbarrows, tractors and lorries.

c. A tidy muck heap will aid rotting, reduce the risk of it becoming a fire hazard and improve the appearance of the yard.

d. Empty the wheelbarrow into the back of the muck heap area or toss the contents of the wheelbarrow on top of the existing muck heap.

e. Using a fork, level and beat down the top of the muck heap, straightening the front as you go. This process is termed "squaring off".

f. As the heap increases in size, it is helpful to climb on top and trample it down.

Muck Heap Disposal

The method of disposal depends upon the size of the muck heap, type of bedding, location and facilities.

a. In some areas, mushroom farmers will remove straw muck heaps for a small fee, providing there is a large enough quantity to make it worthwhile.

b. A well-rotted muck heap may be mixed with farmyard manure and spread on fields as fertiliser. It is not suitable for fertilising grazing for horses because of the likelihood of spreading worm larvae and increasing the worm burden on the field.

c. Small muck heaps can be kept burning, providing the prevailing winds keep the smoke away from the yard and your neighbours.

d. Shavings muck heaps are more difficult to dispose of as they take much longer to rot down.   (20 minutes)

Follow-up Work

1. Students should be watched and corrected where necessary while mucking out and relaying various types of bedding.

2. Question and answer:

a. Name different types of bedding and give some pros and cons of using each.

b. Name different bedding systems and explain their pros and cons.

c. Why is it important to tie up the horse while mucking out?

d. How should a wheelbarrow be loaded?

e. Describe the mucking out process.

f. Explain how to build and maintain a muck heap.

6 The Field-kept Horse

Time

1 hour 30 minutes

Resources

a. Pictures and samples of types of fencing, poisonous plants, grasses, shelter, watering systems and farm machinery.
b. Handouts.

Location

a. Lecture room.
b. Fields.

Preparation

a. Copy the correct number of handouts for the students attending.
b. Arrange pictures and samples in the lecture room, with OHP/ slide projector if needed.
c. Select the field to be used and note down relevant points to be shown to the students.

Aims

- To teach recognition of poisonous plants, good grazing pasture, suitable fencing, watering systems and shelter.
- To teach how a paddock becomes horse sick.

Objective

- To increase understanding of the horse's needs and what is required in a field suitable for horses.

Starting in the lecture room, work through the following points, using samples and pictures as appropriate.

1. Fencing

General Points

a. The type of fencing you choose depends upon financial constraints, type of horse and existing fencing, hedges, etc.
b. Three rails or strands of wire will discourage horses from reaching through the fence. This reduces the likelihood of broken fences and escape.
c. The bottom rail/wire should be approximately 45 cm (18 in) from the ground. This allows horses to graze immediately under the fence but is too low for them to roll underneath it. If it is any lower than this, horses may get a foot caught over the bottom rail/wire.
d. The top rail/wire should be approximately 135 cm (53 in) high.
e. Posts are placed 5–6 m (5½–6½ yd) apart.
f. For Shetland ponies, you will need to lower these measurements, or use a different type of fencing, as Shetlands would escape easily under the bottom wire.
g. As horses are inclined to lean against fencing, wire and rails should be fixed to the inside of the posts, to prevent them from springing off.

Types of Fencing

- Post and rail — Usually constructed of wood, although other materials, such as metal rails and concrete posts, can be used. Although expensive, post and rail provides a strong visible fence. The wood should be treated with a weatherproof preservative and will last longer if repainted each year.

Some of the problems of using unsuitable fencing

- Post and wire — Less expensive and therefore frequently used. Plain wire is best for horses, although it will stretch when leant on, therefore it should be frequently checked and made taut. Barbed wire may command more respect but poses a problem as it can cause horrific injuries. New Zealand rugs are frequently torn on barbed wire.

  Rail and wire are often combined with a top rail and two lower strands of wire, or a top and bottom rail with a strand of wire between.

- Hedges — Providing they are not poisonous and are checked for poisonous plants, hedges make good natural barriers which prevent horses from leaning against or reaching through the wire/rail with which they can be combined.

- Electric – Initially, electric fencing was unsuitable for horses, as it was thin wire that they tended to run through and so become entangled. Now, reels of plastic fencing, with thin strands of wire running through it, are available. This fencing comes in broad strips and various colours, making it highly visible. It has insulators and joining buckles which make it possible to erect the fencing just like post and rail. It has the advantage that horses will not lean on it.
- Stud fencing – This comes in various forms, the aim being to provide a safe fencing for small, valuable foals and boisterous youngsters. A wire mesh is used, with a close enough weave to prevent small feet from becoming trapped. This may be topped with a strip of rubber fencing which adds visibility and will not cause damage if run into.
- Gates – As an essential part of the fencing, gates should open into the field, which helps to prevent horses from barging out and should be wide enough for farm machinery access. To deter thieves, the top hinge pin should be turned over to prevent the gate from being lifted off its hinges, and the gate should be padlocked at both ends. Choose a latch that locks in place and cannot be opened by the horse.

2. Water

A constant fresh supply must be provided.

- Natural sources – A running stream that comes from an unpolluted source is suitable, providing there is firm standing where the horses can approach. Any natural source that becomes stagnant, comes from a polluted area or has a very muddy approach should be fenced off and not used.
- Self-filling trough – The most convenient way of supplying water to the field. The trough should be positioned away from trees, to prevent leaves and debris falling in, and away from the gate, to prevent crowding in this area, but close enough for easy checking. It should also be well away from the fence to allow the horses to visit the trough without getting trapped, or form part of the fence in order to supply two fields at once.

- Other systems — Various different troughs and buckets can be used and filled manually. The important points to remember are:

a. The trough/bucket must be stable, not easily knocked over.
b. There should be no sharp edges, handles or protrusions that a horse could be injured on.
c. It must be cleaned and topped up frequently.

3. Shelter

Horses need protection from wind and rain in the winter and should be provided with shade in summer.

- Natural — Trees and hedges provide the best form of shelter for large groups of horses. They can then group themselves, without fighting, in the most sheltered or shaded part of the field.
- Man-made — Suitable for smaller groups, they should be positioned to protect horses from the prevailing wind. A three-sided construction allows for easy access, and also escape, through the open side. The shelter should be large enough to accommodate all the horses.

4. Poisonous Plants and Trees

It is important to recognise poisonous plants, not just know their names. It is also helpful to know where they are likely to grow.

Poisonous trees and hedges should be fenced off and kept well cut back to prevent horses reaching them over the fence. Oak trees pose a particular problem, as they drop acorns each autumn. Acorns are relished by many horses and can lead to severe cases of colic. The best policy is to avoid such fields in the autumn. Squirrels will help to clear the acorns, which can also be rolled. This partly crushes them and squashes them into the ground.

Poisonous plants should be pulled up before they go to seed, where possible, to prevent them from spreading. Some, like buttercups, may only be eradicated with the use of weed killers.

J.A.Allen & Co.Ltd.

The Horseman's Publisher

laburnum

yew

foxglove

ragwort

hemlock

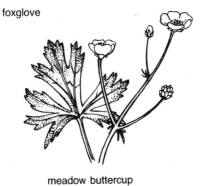

meadow buttercup

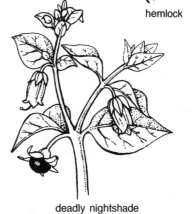

deadly nightshade

Some poisonous plants and trees

Ragwort, the best known of plants poisonous to horses, is rarely eaten when growing. However, when wilted or dried it becomes more palatable but it is still poisonous. It is advisable to burn the plants after pulling them up. Hay should not be made from fields containing ragwort.

Ornamental plants, trees and shrubs are likely to be poisonous. If in doubt, fence them off or remove them. Many of the poisons are accumulative. If your horse eats a plant with no apparent ill effects, it doesn't necessarily mean you should let it go on eating more.

The poisonous plants most commonly found:
- Foxgloves
- Bracken
- Deadly and woody nightshade
- Hemlock
- Ivy
- Ragwort
- Buttercups

Trees
- Yew
- Oak
- Laburnum

Hedges
- Privet
- Laurel
- Rhododendron   (45 minutes)

5. Maintaining Good Pasture

a. Areas of grass that taste sweetest to the horse are grazed very short, like lawns. If the field is overgrazed, these "lawns" become patchy and grazing is ruined for the future. Fields should be rested as the grass gets short, to allow for a period of regrowth. How often, and how long, the field is rested depends upon the number of horses grazing and the speed of regrowth. In spring, given warm weather and rain, the grass will grow rapidly.

b. Horses avoid grazing soured areas of grass where they have left their droppings. This creates a wasted area of long, rough grass. These "roughs" should be topped. This means they are cut short in order to encourage dense growth, rather than sparse areas of long grass that the horses will continue to avoid grazing. If available, sheep and cattle will top the long grass, being less fussy eaters than horses.

c. As well as making the grazing unpalatable to the horse, droppings contain worm larvae which will spread onto the grass, be eaten by the grazing horses and, therefore, increase each horse's worm burden. If the paddock is small, the droppings should be removed daily. As this is not practical in large fields, they should be spread out with a harrow. Once spread, earthworms, rain, dung beetles, etc., will quickly work the droppings into the soil. At the same time the larvae will be exposed to the weather and some may be destroyed before they can be eaten.

   A practical alternative to harrowing is now available, in the form of a large vacuum machine mounted on the back of a Land-Rover or tractor, which vacuums up the droppings.

d. Apart from removing droppings, the worm burden on the field can be reduced by periodically grazing sheep and cattle. They eat the horse worm larvae, which are unable to survive in other animals, thus breaking the cycle and reducing the worm burden.

e. Plants like nettles and thistles will also need to be removed from the field. Although they are not poisonous, they will compete with the grass, leaving your field with more weed than grazing. Again, regular topping and/or grazing sheep and cattle will help to keep these plants, and others like them, under control.

f. Seek advice about fertilisers from an expert, as this may be needed, and should be applied in spring or autumn.

If you *don't* follow these procedures, you will end up with a horse-sick paddock. This is a paddock with obvious lawns and roughs, an excess amount of droppings, bare and poached areas and weeds and poisonous plants in abundance, and it will carry a very heavy worm burden.

(15 minutes)

6. Daily Checks

The grass-kept horse and its field must be checked several times every day. It only takes a few moments for a piece of fencing to be broken or for one horse to kick and injure another. Either of these incidents could have dire results if left unchecked for any length of time. Early-morning and late-evening checks are essential, as the horse will have been, or will be, left unseen through the night period. Throughout the day, look in on the horse as frequently as possible.

  a. Check that the horse is behaving normally, shows no signs of ill health and has not sustained any injuries. Pick out its feet and check the shoes.
  b. If the horse is rugged, check that the fastenings are secure, replace the rug if it has slipped, look for tears and check that the rug is dry inside.
  c. Look at the fencing and gate. Are they secure?
  d. Is the water supply flowing and clean?
  e. Look for poisonous plants and weeds, especially in the spring.
  f. Make sure no debris has found its way into the field. There may be a tin can, plastic bag, etc., that needs removing.
  g. Shelters should be checked in case of broken boards or maybe a hole in the roof.   (10 minutes)

7. Practice

Now take the students to the field to look at and discuss the fencing, water supply, grazing, shelter, poisonous plants and general suitability of the field for grazing horses.   (20 minutes)

Follow-up Work

1. The students should be observed putting theory into practice, checking fields and field-kept horses.
2. Use question and answer sessions to confirm knowledge:

   a. Why should the bottom rail or wire of a fence, be approximately 45 cm (18 in) from the ground?
   b. What different forms of fencing are there?
   c. Why is barbed wire not a good fencing for horses?
   d. Which way should gates open and how should they be secured, with thieves in mind?
   e. Are natural sources of water suitable for horses?
   f. What forms of shelter may be available for grass-kept horses and what do they need sheltering from?
   g. Name and describe six poisonous plants or trees.
   h. What does a horse-sick paddock look like?
   i. Why is it important to make daily checks? How often should they be made and what do you check?

7   The Healthy Horse

Time

2 hours 20 minutes

Resources

a. A horse in good health, that can also be led in hand at walk and trot.
b. A horse, or pictures of horses, not in good health.
c. Samples of worming powders/paste/liquid.
d. Samples of wound powders and creams.

Location

First the lecture room, then the stable yard.

Preparation

a. Choose the horse in good health and select a suitable yard area for it to be tied up in. Have its bridle available for leading it in hand.
b. Collect samples of wormers and wound powder, etc., and arrange these in the lecture room.
c. Set up pictures and OHP or slide projector if needed.

Aims

- To teach how to recognise when a horse is or is not in good health.

- To teach ways of preventing disease and how to give basic first aid to the horse.
- To teach what records to keep in relation to the horse's health.
- To teach how to care for a sick horse.

Objectives

- To improve understanding of the care of the horse and raise standards of care.

Starting in the lecture room, work through the following points, using samples and pictures as appropriate.

1. Signs of the Horse Being in Good Health

- It should be "well covered" or "well furnished". This means having enough muscle and fat on its body to cover its skeletal frame in such a way that there are no prominent bony areas.
- The horse is alert, with ears mobile.
- Eating and drinking normally.
- Salmon-pink mucous membranes.
- Supple skin, moving easily over the body.
- A shine to the coat.
- No abnormal heat or swellings.
- Droppings should break as they hit the ground, and be green or golden in colour depending upon the feed eaten. Horses pass droppings eight to ten times a day.
- Urine should be pale yellow.
- Normal temparature: 100–101°F or 38°C.
- Normal pulse 35–45 beats per minute; higher for foals, varying between 50–100 beats per minute.
- Normal respiration: 8–12 in and out breaths per minute. (All of the above taken at rest.)
- Able to carry its weight evenly on all four feet.
- No sign of discharge from nose or eyes. Eyes fully open.
- When a skin recoil test is made (that is, the skin on the neck is pinched between thumb and first finger), the skin should recoil immediately, demonstrating its elasticity.

- Normal response to capillary refill test. This is tested by pressing the gum with your thumb, which restricts the flow of blood. When you remove your thumb, the capillaries should immediately refill with blood.

2. How to Take TPR (Temperature, Pulse, Respiration)

a. Temperature − Shake down the mercury in the thermometer, or zero the reading on a digital model. Grease the bulb end with a small amount of Vaseline. While an assistant holds its head, stand to one side of the horse's hind quarters and hold its tail to one side. Insert the greased, bulb end into the rectum using a rotating action. The inserted section should be angled to rest against the wall of the rectum in order to give a true reading. Take care to hold the thermometer firmly to prevent it from being drawn into the rectum. Remove after one minute, wipe clean and read.

b. Pulse − Press your fingers (not a thumb) gently against the artery located on the lower jaw or inside the foreleg, just in front of the elbow. Use a watch with a second hand and time how many pulse beats there are in 30 seconds, then double this number for the total beats per minute.

c. Respiration − Watch the horse's flanks and count the in and out movement of inhalation and exhalation together as one. Time the breaths for 30 seconds, and double the figure for the total breaths per minute.

3. Signs of the Horse Being Unwell

- If any one, or all of these are prominent: ribs/hips/croup/backbone, or if the top of the neck is sunken away, then the horse is underweight.
- Not alert, head low and ears unresponsive.
- Not eating or drinking usual amounts.
- Mucous membranes may be yellow (indicating jaundice and disruption of the liver), pale (indicating anaemia, probably

due to infection) or blue (indicating lack of oxygen, due to poor circulation).

- Skin appears taut. When the skin recoil test is made, the pinched skin stands proud, being slow to recoil.
- The coat is dull and staring.
- Abnormal areas of heat and swelling.
- Droppings may be loose, or very hard, and/or irregular.
- Urine red/brown or black.
- TPR may be raised or lowered: temperature more than 1°F, or 0.5°C above or below normal. Pulse raised or lowered. Respiration shallow and rapid.
- Showing unlevel steps.
- Discharge from the nostrils or eyes.
- Eyes not fully open and/or third eyelid showing.
- Blood slow to return to capillaries after refill test.
- Showing signs of discomfort; for example, pacing round the box, looking round at, or kicking at, belly, frequently getting up and lying down, pawing the ground, trying to stale and failing, patchy sweat, "tucked up".
- Excessively overweight.

Finally, as each horse will have its own distinct habits and behaviour patterns, make sure you know your horse well. In this way you will notice the slightest abnormality that may indicate ill health. Act immediately if you notice something is amiss. Report to the yard manager or call the vet. Quick responses may limit the spread of disease, reduce the need for lengthy treatment and keep the horse's suffering to a minimum.   (30 minutes)

4. Practice

Now, in the stable yard, the students can take turns to indicate and describe to you all the points of good health and also what they would see if the horse was in poor health, using the horse you have selected. You should demonstrate the skin recoil and capillary refill tests and how to take TPR.   (20 minutes)

Return to the lecture room.

5. Preventive Measures

It is important to incorporate regular inspections into your daily routine. While working around the horses, you must constantly observe them. First thing in the morning, however, the horses will have been unobserved for many hours, therefore this first inspection is vital.

Check water supplies, rugs and signs of health, making sure the horses are safe, happy and healthy. The same applies before and after a lunch break and especially last thing at night when you must make every effort to ensure the horses are securely and safely rugged and stabled with a plentiful water supply. Do the same for your grass-kept horses. In this way, many accidents/illnesses can be avoided.

Apart from good general stable management, various types of routine health care are important in the prevention of ill health.

- Worming – All horses carry a worm burden. However, an excessive amount will cause disruption of the digestive system, damage to internal organs and general ill health. If untreated, the horse may die. To keep the worm burden low, horses should be "wormed" with a recognised brand of wormer on a regular basis. Worm every four to six weeks if your horse is grazing with many other horses on infrequently rested pasture. Worm every six to eight weeks if your horse is stabled and or grazing with few other horses on well-rested pasture that is also grazed by cattle/sheep.

  Wormers are available in the form of powder/granules, paste and liquid. Different brands will destroy different species of worm. Some worms may become resistant to various brands so it is advisable to change your brand once or twice yearly. Ask your vet for advice. The wormer may be fed to the horse in its feed but many dislike the taste and refuse to eat it. Paste and liquid may be squirted directly into the horse's mouth by means of a large syringe. There is usually a guide to dosage on the syringe, which you preset before inserting into the corner of the horse's mouth (where there are no teeth) then press the plunger, aiming the dose as far towards the back of the tongue as possible. This needs to be one very quick movement!

Worming the horse

- Teeth — The horse's top jaw is wider than its bottom jaw. As the horse masticates and its teeth wear down, sharp edges develop on the outer edge of the upper set of molars and also on the inner edge of the lower set. These sharp edges can cut into the horse's cheeks when it is eating or wearing tack. Some of the feed, especially hay and grass, may be partly

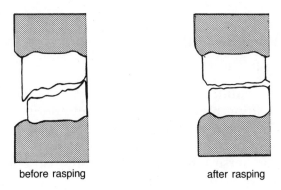

before rasping   after rasping

The teeth should be checked about twice a year

chewed and then spat out because of the discomfort. This is called quidding. When ridden, the horse may resist the bit or drool from one side of its mouth.

A vet, or horse dentist, should visit and check teeth approximately twice a year. He or she will examine the mouth and rasp off sharp edges if necessary, as well as checking for loose, chipped or infected teeth. If sharp teeth are left unattended, the horse will suffer from poor digestion and loss of condition.

- Vaccinations — Horses should be vaccinated against tetanus and given a booster injection every two years. They should also be vaccinated against equine influenza, for which a booster must be given yearly.   (15 minutes)

6. Health Records

In order to keep track of vet's visits, worming dates, etc., a record should be kept for each horse, perhaps in the form of a chart, including the dates of:

- Last worming dose and type of wormer used.
- When teeth were checked and next date due.
- When 'flu and tetanus vaccinations were given, and when next due.
- When last shod and date of next farrier's visit.
- The last vet's visit and why the vet attended.   (10 minutes)

7. When to Call the Vet

Call the vet if:

- A wound is bleeding profusely, is more than skin deep or is spurting blood (indicating a cut artery).
- The horse exhibits mild signs of colic for more than half an hour or if it exhibits any violent signs of colic.
- The horse's temperature is more than one degree F higher or lower than normal.
- If the horse is lame.

- If the horse is coughing repeatedly and not clearing its nostrils after coughing.
- If in doubt call the vet. It is better to be safe than sorry!

A horse suffering from any of the above should not be worked. This may seem obvious but there have been cases where, for example, a horse has shown symptoms of mild colic which then appear to cease. The horse has been ridden soon after and had another colic attack, with the rider on board; or a slightly lame horse has been ridden, the lameness appears to wear off but after work the horse has been much lamer than before. So, wait for veterinary advice.   (10 minutes)

8. Minor Wounds

a. Many minor wounds can be treated without veterinary assistance, providing you have a first-aid kit, including:

- Hose and cold water supply.
- Scissors.
- Cotton wool.
- Salt.
- Warm water.
- Clean bowl.
- Wound powder/cream.
- Antiseptic spray.
- Gamgee.

b. Bruising is accompanied by heat and swelling. This can be effectively reduced by cold hosing, especially if the bruising is on the leg. To make sure you do not frighten the horse, start with a trickle of water, and gradually move the trickle from the foot up the horse's leg to the damaged area. The water pressure can then be increased. If there is an open wound with the bruising, hosing will help remove the mud etc., and clean the wound. Hose above an open wound, to allow the water to trickle over it. Do not hose directly onto an open wound.

c. Bleeding may be stopped by applying direct pressure to the wound with a clean pad.

d. Once bleeding has ceased, any hair overlapping the wound should be carefully trimmed away. This will help you to see the extent of the wound.

e. Warm, salty water works as a safe and mild antiseptic with which you can clean the wound. (Use 1 teaspoon of salt to ½ litre/1 pt of boiled, then cooled, water.)

f. Dip cotton wool into the salty water and clean the wound, working from the middle outwards. Be careful not to rub grit into the wound and use a fresh piece of cotton wool for each wipe, never returning a dirty piece of cotton wool to the clean salt water, nor to the wound.

g. Dry the wound and then apply wound powder, spray or cream.

h. This procedure can be followed for all minor wounds, whether it is a saddle sore, scratch, kick, etc. Hosing can only really be used on the lower part of the body, as higher up would involve soaking a large part of the horse, which would certainly be inappropriate in cold weather.   (15 minutes)

9. Nursing a Sick Horse

a. The horse should have very frequent visits to check that there is no deterioration in its condition but visits should be made with a minimum of disturbance.

b. A regular check should be made and written records kept of its TPR and other general points to do with its condition; for example how much it is eating, if there is more or less swelling, whether the horse is lying down more or less, etc.

c. Remove droppings frequently and keep the bed level, with good high banks. Short straw, or shavings, allow for ease of movement. Shavings will stick into wounds and should be avoided for this type of ailment. Full mucking out may not be possible if the horse has limited movement. Use the deep litter system in this case.

d. Keep the stable well ventilated but free from draughts.

e. Keep the horse warm but not weighed down with heavy clothing. Use leg bandages, and possibly a hood, to keep extremities warm. Use light, quilted rugs.

f. Do not groom vigorously if the horse is weak. Pick out the feet twice daily. Sponge eyes, nose and under the dock each day. Lightly brush over, being careful not to let the horse get cold.

g. If worn, remove bandages daily and hand massage the legs to improve the circulation.

h. Monitor how much water is drunk and keep the supply very fresh.

i. Give light, tempting but laxative feeds. Remove any uneaten food immediately. Stale food and water will discourage the horse and possibly delay recovery.

j. Follow veterinary instructions carefully.

k. If the horse has an eye injury, keep the stable darkened and avoid bright lights.

l. Unless the vet advises otherwise, give an ad lib supply of hay.   (15 minutes)

10. How to Recognise Lameness

a. When lame in a front limb/foot, the horse will be reluctant to put its weight on the lame leg. In order to keep as much weight as possible off this leg, the horse will raise its head up as it puts this leg to the ground. When it puts its sound leg to the ground, it will put extra weight on it and drop its head down as it does so.

b. Walking straight towards you, on firm level ground, you may observe the head and neck of the sound horse bobbing gently in rhythm with the walk. Trotting straight towards you, the head and neck of the sound horse will be held level.

c. If you watch the head and neck of a horse that is lame in a front limb, in either walk or trot, you will notice it raise its head high when the lame leg comes to the ground and drop its head low when the sound leg comes to the ground.

d. The extent to which the horse raises and lowers its head will depend upon the degree of lameness, varying from a slight nod to a very pronounced movement up and down.

e. Hind leg lameness can be more difficult to detect. Watching a sound horse from behind, the hind quarters should rise and fall evenly as the horse walks or trots away from you on a straight line.

   f. A horse that is lame behind will drop one quarter lower and raise one quarter higher. This may be difficult to see if the lameness is only slight.

In the stable yard, walk and trot the horse in a straight line, on firm level ground, while the students observe and pay special attention to the steadiness of the head and neck and the evenness of the quarters going up and down.   (25 minutes)

Follow-up Work

1. Students can only practise treating wounds, observation of ill health, detecting lameness, etc., as and when they occur. Involvement should be encouraged whenever possible, in order that they can gain experience.
2. Students should watch worming doses being administered and teeth being checked, then practise themselves under supervision.
3. Question and answer sessions:

   a. List six points that show your horse is in good health, and six that show poor health.
   b. Point out, on a demonstration horse, where it would be lacking fat and muscle if it was underweight.
   c. How often should a horse be wormed and how is this done?
   d. How often, and why, should your horse's teeth be checked?
   e. What health records should you keep?
   f. What vaccinations should your horse have?
   g. How do you treat a minor skin wound?
   h. List six points that are important in the nursing of sick horses.
   i. How do you tell if a horse is lame?
   j. What should the normal TPR of the horse be?
   k. How do you take TPR?

8 Psychology

Time

1 hour 10 minutes

Resources

a. Video of horses demonstrating instinctive behaviour.
b. Any horse available to you that may demonstrate relevant behaviour patterns.

Location

Lecture room.

Preparation

a. Think of, and list, examples of horses known to the students that demonstrate some of the behaviour patterns you will be discussing.
b. Set up video and television.

Aims

- To teach students the natural instincts of the horse.
- To teach students how the horse adapts and behaves in captivity.

Objective

- To improve the students' understanding of horses, thereby helping the students to work more safely and effectively with them.

65

1. Natural Instincts and Life Style

Discuss some of the horse's natural instincts and behaviour patterns, using the video where appropriate.

a. The basic instincts to survive and reproduce govern the behaviour of the horse. The strongest, most dominant stallion will gather a group of mares and endeavour to protect them. There will also be a dominant mare who will lead the group.

b. Horses are sociable animals, living together as a herd. Led by the dominant mare and stallion, stronger or weaker members of the herd will establish their place, resulting in an order similar to the "pecking order" among chickens. Many smaller groups of "friends" will also form within the herd.

c. Horses are not predatory animals, but would have been preyed upon in the wild. They instinctively flee from danger, using their speed to escape from their attacker. It is important that the whole herd should keep together if danger threatens, therefore if one horse takes flight, the whole herd will respond and go too.

d. The horse's sense of hearing is very acute. Their mobile ears constantly move to listen for danger that may approach from any direction. Likewise, their eyes are set on the sides of their faces for good peripheral vision. They have a small blind spot immediately behind and in front of them, but can move their heads around in order to see if predators are approaching. The horse's head and ear movements are a constant indication of what it is thinking and feeling.

e. If cornered and unable to take flight, the horse will try to defend itself. It can turn its hind legs towards the attacker and lash out or it can bite and strike out with a foreleg.

f. Horses graze throughout the day, keeping the stomach supplied with food but never letting it become full. This enables them to take flight at any time without having the restriction of a full stomach pressing against their lungs.

g. Horses rest by sleeping on their feet. Again, they can quickly take flight from this position. However, if the weather is fine and the sun shining, they like to lie down, providing there is no imminent threat of danger. One or more members of the group will remain standing, as lookouts for the "herd".

h. All horses enjoy rolling. It helps to remove old winter coat and camouflages the horse by covering it in mud.

i. A horse can scratch many parts of its body with its teeth. However, as it cannot reach its own withers, it will approach and scratch the withers of another horse. This will stimulate the other horse into reciprocal scratching.

j. Colts and fillies will be boisterous together. Through play they learn about adult behaviour and mutual respect.

k. Older horses will tolerate playful youngsters unless they become particularly boisterous. They may then bite or kick to establish their superiority and put the youngster "in its place".

(20 minutes)

2. How the Horse Adapts to Being a Domestic Animal

In the Field

In many ways field-kept horses have a fairly natural life style.

a. They will take flight as a herd if danger threatens.

b. They will take turns lying down and keeping watch.

c. They will form smaller groups of "friends" within a large group.

d. They will establish who is the strongest and therefore the leader.

e. When relaxed, they will be seen grazing, spread out across the field, standing nose to tail swishing flies from each other's faces or scratching each other's withers.

f. Mares and geldings should be separated in the spring and summer. This helps to prevent injuries occurring when geldings begin to behave like stallions by singling out mares in season, and fighting with each other.

g. After its companions have been taken away a horse left on its own in the field, may panic. It will call, trot up and down the fence and possibly try to jump out, as instinct tells it to follow the herd. However, horses soon adjust to being taken in and out of the field, providing more than one is left behind for company.

h. One young and one old horse kept together may not enjoy each other's company. The young one will want to play, which may bother the older horse. However, several youngsters kept together will play happily, while older horses graze and rest quietly.

i. In wet and windy weather, or when hot and bothered by flies, the horses will group together in sheltered areas.

j. In the confines of the field, a stronger horse may corner a weaker member of the group and defensive behaviour will be seen. The horses will kick out at each other or use their teeth to bite. Those with a more timid nature may try to jump out of the field rather than defend themselves.

k. If a new horse is introduced to an established group, there will be a period of adjustment. This horse will have to establish its place in the herd. If it is quite dominant in nature there may be a lot of fighting if it challenges the leaders of the herd. If it is more timid in nature, it will probably settle quite quickly, not posing a threat to any of the others. Initially, the rest of the herd will gather together and approach the new arrival. They will smell each other and there is likely to be kicking, squealing and some cantering around. The new arrival will also spend some time exploring its new surroundings. It will take at least a day to settle in.

l. If a horse has, for some reason, been stabled for a long period, it will take great delight in being returned to the more natural environment of the field. Typical behaviour includes galloping, rolling, exploring the field, smelling droppings left by other horses, bucking, snorting and, with all senses alert, surveying its new surroundings.   (20 minutes)

In the Stable

This is a most unnatural environment for the horse.

a. Confined to a stable, the horse cannot take flight if threatened. Its only option is to defend itself by biting or kicking. To prevent this dangerous behaviour, it is very important that we handle the horse in a quiet, kind and confident manner, making it feel safe and relaxed in its stable.

b. Being separated from the herd can lead to stable vices like weaving and box walking but careful planning can help to make the horse feel more relaxed. For example, American barn stabling allows the horses to see and smell each other so they continue to feel like part of a herd.

c. When we restrict its intake of feed the horse's need to be almost constantly grazing may lead to vices like crib biting and wind sucking. By feeding little and often, with as constant a supply of hay/carrots/swede as possible for the horse to nibble, we can minimise these problems.

d. The horse's acute hearing will pick up anything happening around the yard. However, when confined to the stable it may not be able to see what is causing the noise. This may lead to the horse fretting and becoming nervous. For this reason, keep noise and disturbance to a minimum.

e. Consider the horse's temperament when deciding where to stable it. A stallion will want to see all activity as horses leave and enter the yard so that he feels he is watching over his herd. A timid horse may be miserable stabled between two very dominant horses. Horses lacking confidence will fret if stabled where they can constantly see other horses leaving the yard, as this will make them feel that the herd is leaving without them.   (15 minutes)

When Being Ridden

When handling horses, we take the place of the leader of the herd. If the horse is confident in us as its leader, it will do as we ask. When it loses confidence in us, problems begin.

a. When the horse is being ridden out alone, or at the front of the ride, it will go forward happily if it has confidence in its rider. Although he or she is sitting on the horse's back, the rider is still the leader and the horse must have trust in him or her. If the horse doesn't trust us, it may nap by refusing to go forward or by spinning round, running backwards, etc.

b. When being ridden through the countryside your horse will be on a constant look out for danger. Bushes, hedges and banks could all be places where a predator may be hiding, therefore it may be reluctant to approach or may try to give such things a wide berth. A confident rider will reassure the horse by riding forward calmly but firmly. Hitting or shouting at the horse will only worry it and make the problem worse.

c. As always, a frightened horse will try to take flight. If it is in pain it will be afraid, therefore pulling at the reins, using badly fitting tack or an unbalanced rider are all problems likely to cause the horse to rush forward, jog or buck in an attempt to get free.

d. The herd instinct will lead to problems if you try to separate horses while out on a hack. Likewise, if one horse shies at an object, all the other horses will shy too.

Most problems with horses can be understood, and solved, by considering the horse's natural life style and instincts. This will lead you to the cause of the problem. Once the cause has been understood, the solution will be easy to find.   (15 minutes)

Follow-up Work

1. Observe students in their day-to-day handling of horses in different situations and question them about the horse's behaviour as situations arise.
2. Question and answer sessions will help to confirm their knowledge:

    a. Name four basic instincts of the horse.
    b. Describe four situations in which you have seen these instincts demonstrated.
    c. Explain the importance of handling horses kindly and calmly.
    d. When a new horse is introduced to others, what behaviour are you likely to see?
    e. How would a horse behave if left on its own in the field?
    f. How can we make the environment of the stabled horse as natural as possible?
    g. What behaviour problems may we see if we do not consider the needs of the stabled horse?

9 Saddlery: its Use, Care and Fitting

Time

3 hours

Resources

a. GP saddle and snaffle bridle.
b. Flash, drop and cavesson nosebands.
c. Lunge cavesson and side reins.
d. Breastplate, martingales and brushing boots.
e. Suitable selection of horses to fit the tack on.
f. Tack cleaning equipment.
g. Selection of bits.
h. Handouts.

Location

Lecture room or tack room and then the stable yard.

Preparation

a. Copy the correct number of handouts for the students attending.
b. Gather equipment in the lecture room or tack room.
c. Tie up the horses in your selected area.

Aims

- To teach recognition, purpose and fit of various items of tack in everyday use.
- To teach how to clean and care for this tack.

Objectives

- To enable students to fit tack correctly and thereby prevent injuries from ill-fitting equipment.
- To improve awareness of safety by learning how to care for equipment.

1. Points of the Saddle and Bridle

Starting in the lecture room or tack room, work through the points of the saddle and bridle.   (15 minutes)

Move on to the stable yard and demonstrate the correct tacking up procedure.

2. Tacking Up Procedure

Most tacking up, fastening of buckles, etc., is conducted from the near side of the horse. In this way, there is less need to keep passing from one side of the horse to the other, which might unsettle it.

The Saddle

a. Either first place the numnah separately on the horse's back or attach it to the saddle and then place both saddle and numnah together well forward over the withers (in order to keep the hair lying flat) and slide back into place, just behind the shoulders.
b. The girth may already have been attached on one side and will have been laid over the top of the saddle. It can now be let down, taking care not to let it drop and bang against the horse's legs.
c. Check that the numnah is smooth under the saddle and that it has been lifted well up into the gullet, to prevent it from putting pressure on the spine.

FOR LECTURING PURPOSES

pommel

waist

seat

cantle

D ring

saddle tree

lining
(part of panel)

skirt

stirrup bar

stirrup iron

stirrup leather

girth

saddle flap

webbing

point pocket

thigh roll

gullet

lining

panel

knee
roll

buckle
guard

girth
straps

panel

The points of the saddle

J.A. Allen & Co. Ltd.
The Horseman's Publisher

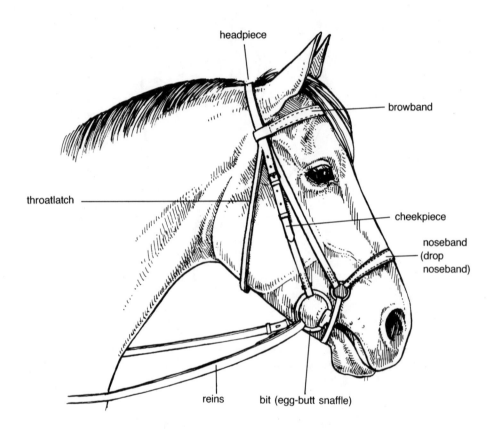

headpiece

browband

throatlatch

cheekpiece

noseband
(drop
noseband)

reins

bit (egg-butt snaffle)

The points of the bridle

J.A. Allen & Co. Ltd.

The Horseman's Publisher

Two designs of safety iron

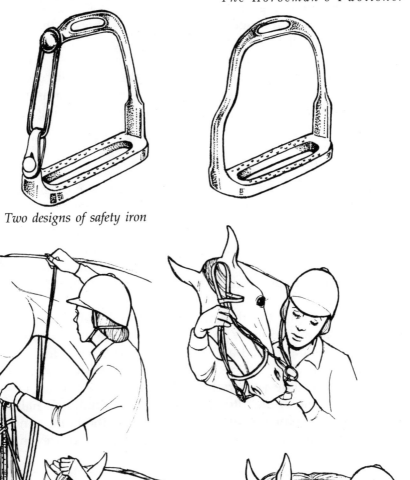

The correct procedure for putting on the bridle

    d. Do up the girth on the other side. Pull it up gently, not making it too tight too quickly. Most horses tense against the girth as it is done up. When they relax again, the girth becomes loose and will need further adjustment.

    e. After checking and tightening the girth, lift each foreleg in turn and pull it forward. This action smooths the hair and skin under the girth, so avoiding any pinching.

The Bridle

The horse's head is a very sensitive area. All movements required for putting on the bridle should be gentle, while positive control is maintained.

    a. Untie the horse, place the rope over its neck, and remove the head collar. Buckle the head collar around the horse's neck, where it can be used to restrain the horse if it tries to move away.

    b. Check that the throatlatch and noseband have been undone. Hold the bridle in your left hand while you put the reins over the horse's head and place them well back down its neck.

    c. Stand with your right shoulder under the horse's chin, and gently slide your right hand around the horse's nose.

    d. Pass the bridle into your right hand, holding it halfway down the cheekpieces, and lift the bit up to the horse's mouth. (This right hand also rests gently on the nose to prevent the horse from raising its head too high.)

    e. With thumb and first finger of the left hand, push the bit gently into the horse's mouth, while you use your two middle fingers to open its mouth. (Your fingers should slide into the mouth in the gap between the two sets of teeth.)

    f. Once the bit is in position, keep the bridle lifted with the right hand, to prevent the bit from slipping out again. Take hold of the headpiece with the left hand and gently push the offside ear forward underneath it with the right hand. Push the nearside ear into place in the same way.

    g. Check that the forelock and mane are smoothly separated under the headpiece, then secure the throatlatch and noseband.

Accessories

a. Boots can be put on before the saddle and bridle.
b. The breastplate/martingale can be slipped over the horse's head before putting the saddle on. The girth can then be slipped straight through the breastplate/martingale loop.
c. Side reins can be attached as soon as the saddle has been secured. They should be left clipped to the D rings.
d. The lunge cavesson is slipped on after the bridle, using the same procedure for pushing the ears gently forward under the headpiece.   (20 minutes)

3. Fitting the Equipment

Demonstrate how to check the fitting of the equipment.

GP Saddle

The tree, around which the saddle is built, is made in various widths, usually narrow, medium and wide. Saddles are also made with different lengths of seat, to accommodate various sizes of rider. The saddle should be fitted without a numnah then girthed up with the horse standing level.

a. When placed on the horse's back, there must be a clear passage down the gullet. No weight should be taken on the horse's spine.
b. There should be approximately a 10-cm (4 in) clearance between the pommel and the withers, without the rider.
c. The saddle should be level, neither too low at the front nor at the back, which would tip the rider forwards or backwards.
d. The full surface area of the panels should be in contact with the horse's back. These will distribute the rider's weight over the largest possible area.
e. The length of the saddle should suit the length of the horse's back. There should not be any weight on the loins.
f. The knee roll, panels and saddle flap should not protrude

over the shoulder, as they may restrict the horse's freedom of movement.

g. The fitting of the saddle is not complete until seen with the rider. The rider's weight will reduce the amount of clearance over the withers and spine.   (20 minutes)

Snaffle Bridle

Bridles are made in different sizes: pony, cob and full size. There are also different widths and strengths of leather. For example, bridles for heavyweight horses and hunters will be made of strong, broad strips of leather, while bridles for show ponies will be made from finer leather.

a. The job of the browband is to keep the headpiece from slipping back down the horse's neck. It should not pull the headpiece forward, where it will rub, but should keep it in place just behind the ears.

b. The throatlatch, which is attached to the headpiece, has the job of stopping the bridle being pulled off over the horse's ears. It should not be tight when the horse flexes at the poll. When correctly adjusted, you should be able to fit the width of your hand between the horse's cheek and the throatlatch.

c. Apart from having the throatlatch attached to it, the headpiece also supports the cheekpieces.

d. The cheekpieces have the job of supporting the bit, and should be long or short enough to enable you to adjust the bit to the correct level.

e. The reins are attached to the bit to give the rider control. They should not be too short, which may cause the rider to let go if the horse suddenly snatches its head down, nor should they be too long, which may lead to them becoming tangled around the rider's foot.

f. The job of the **cavesson noseband** is as a point of attachment for a standing martingale. However, it is often worn just to make the bridle look complete. It should sit the width of two fingers below the projecting cheek bones, and be loose around the nose to allow free movement of the jaws. Allow for the width of two fingers between the front of the horse's nose and the noseband.

g. The job of the **drop noseband** is to keep the horse's jaws closed. Because of this it is fitted firmly but must not be tight around the soft part of the nose. To be effective, it should be fitted the width of your hand above the upper edge of the horse's nostrils, and be buckled around and under the bit.

h. The job of the **flash noseband** is similar to the drop but it secures the jaw in two places. Its upper strap, which should be thick and padded, is fitted in the same position as the cavesson noseband but is made firm, rather than being left loose. The lower strap is fitted firmly around and under the bit.

i. The snaffle bit should be adjusted to a height where it wrinkles the corners of the horse's mouth. The mouthpiece should not protrude more than 6 mm (¼ in) on either side of the horse's mouth, nor should the bit rings appear to pinch inwards. If the bit is too wide, it will slide from side to side when the rider uses the reins. If it is too narrow, it will pinch and rub the sides of the mouth.   (20 minutes)

Martingales

a. The neck straps of both the standing and running martingale should fit around the base of the neck, allowing for the width of one hand to be placed between the neck and the neck strap.

b. To fit the **standing martingale**, place the neck strap over the horse's head and attach one end to the girth. Then follow the line of the underside of the horse's neck with the martingale strap, up under its throat and down to its chin groove.

c. To fit the **running martingale**, place the strap over the horse's neck and attach the end to the girth. If both rings are drawn back along the line of the shoulder, they should be approximately 15–20 cm (6–8 in) short of reaching the withers.

d. **Rein stops** must be worn with the running martingale. They will prevent the rings from becoming stuck where the reins buckle onto the bit.

e. Both martingales have the job of preventing the horse from raising its head too high: the standing type by exerting pressure

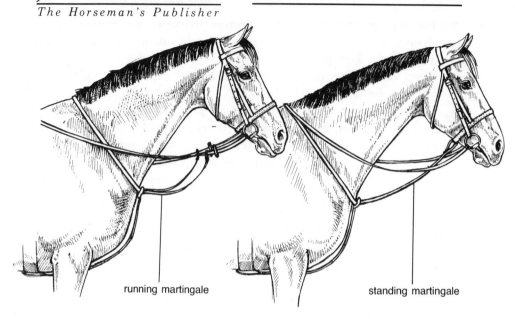

running martingale

standing martingale

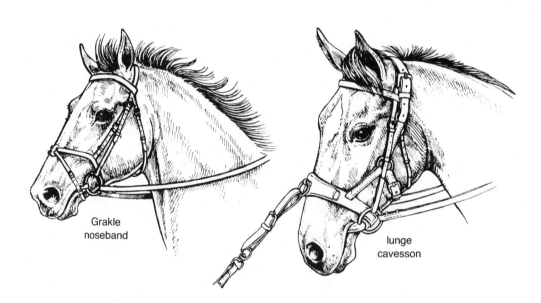

Grakle
noseband

lunge
cavesson

The fitting of accessories

on the nose via the cavesson noseband; the running type by exerting pressure on the reins, which is then transferred to the bit.

f. The running martingale will only work if the rider has a contact on the reins.

g. Both types of martingale should allow the horse free movement of the head and neck while working on the flat or over fences. They should only come into action when the horse tries to raise its head too high for the rider to maintain control.

Breastplate

a. Both hunting and racing style breastplates should fit securely in order to fulfil their job of preventing the saddle from slipping back.

b. Allow for the width of an upright hand between the withers and the wither/neck strap of both styles.

c. The racing style should fit close to the chest, without restricting the shoulder movement.

d. The hunting style should follow the line of the horse's shoulder blades, with the centre ring sitting at the base of the neck in the middle of the chest.

e. The strap from the chest to the girth should hang 3–6 cm (1–2½ in) below the horse's chest.

f. A running or standing martingale attachment can be used with the hunting style breastplate and with some designs of racing breastplates. Simply attach and then fit in the same way as described for the martingales.   (20 minutes)

Lunge Cavesson

a. Because of the force exerted on the lunge cavesson by the lunge line, it must be fitted firmly, hence the need for plenty of padding around the nosepiece.

b. The headpiece and browband (which is optional) should fit as described for the snaffle bridle.

c. The nosepiece should be fitted at the same height as a cavesson noseband (which is normally removed if the bridle is being worn), but should be firmly buckled, without pinching, to prevent the lunge cavesson from slipping.

    d. The throatlatch, which is fitted lower than on the snaffle bridle, is buckled firmly around the lower half of the horse's cheeks. It also helps to stop the lunge cavesson from slipping.

    e. If being used, the bridle should be put on first, with the lunge cavesson placed on top. Then put the throatlatch and nosepiece under the cheekpieces of the bridle. This prevents the lunge cavesson from interfering with the action of the bit.

       Some designs of lunge cavesson may not fit under the bridle cheekpieces without pulling them out of line. In this case, place the throatlatch over the bridle and the nosepiece underneath.

       If the noseband is removed from the bridle, there will be more room for the lunge cavesson to sit comfortably.

Side reins

These come in various different, adjustable designs.

    a. Attach the loop end on each side of the horse by slotting the second or third girth strap through it. Then pass the side rein under the first girth strap.

    b. Once attached to the girth strap, hold each side rein in a straight line towards the horse's bit. While the horse is standing at rest with its head held in a relaxed position, the side reins should just reach the bit. This guideline gives a good starting point to work from. Subsequent adjustment depends on how the horse is then worked on the lunge.

    c. When not in use, the side reins can be hooked onto the D rings of the saddle.   (15 minutes)

Boots

These come in many varied designs for different uses, and are made from a variety of materials. The following general points will apply to the fitting of most boots.

J.A. Allen & Co. Ltd.
The Horseman's Publisher

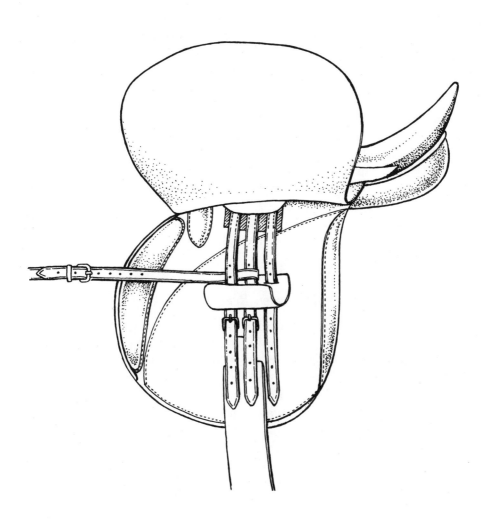

The correct way to attach a side rein to the girth strap

a. The boot should not sit too high, where it may rub the back of the knee or front of the hock when the joint is flexed. It should not sit so low that it rubs the heels when the foot is moving.

b. A firm fit is required to prevent boots from slipping down the leg.

c. With most designs, straps are secured by being drawn firmly across the cannon bone and fastened pointing towards the rear. This helps to prevent unnecessary tension across the tendons.

d. To make them easy to put on and take off, boots are fastened on the outside of the leg. This also helps to prevent knocks against the opposite limb.

e. Fasten the centre strap first to secure the boot. If the horse begins to fidget before the other straps are fastened the boot will then remain in place.

f. Likewise, if the centre strap is unfastened last, the boot will not slip or flap if the horse fidgets when it is taken off.

(15 minutes)

Points to Remember when Removing Tack

a. When removing the bridle, start by undoing the noseband. This is essential if a drop or flash noseband is used, due to its firm fitting. Then undo the throatlatch. Push the headpiece gently forward over the horse's ears. Lower the bridle slowly, in order to allow the horse to drop the bit in its own time. If you pull the bridle away quickly, the bit could catch on the horse's teeth. The horse may then be nervous of having its bridle removed in future.

b. When removing the saddle, let the girth down gently. If it is dropped down, it will bang against the horse's legs and can cause injury as well as frightening the horse. Then lift the saddle up, slightly back and towards you. In this way you avoid pulling against the horse's spine, which would cause bruising and discomfort.

c. When returning from a long hack or a day's hunting, it is a good idea to dismount before reaching home and loosen your horse's girth. This allows the circulation under the saddle to return gradually and avoids a sudden rush of blood (and therefore congestion) to the saddle area.

d. Secure the horse before you remove the tack. Put the head collar around its neck, remove the bridle, then slip the head collar on and tie up. Now remove saddle and boots. To remove a martingale, the girth needs to be undone. In this case, tie up with the head collar over the bridle and remove the saddle first.   (10 minutes)

Return to the lecture/tack room to complete the lecture.

4. Bitting

The following basic principles of bitting should enable you to assess the action of almost any type of bit. In general, we aim to school the horse in such a way that it will respond to the simplest form of bitting.

a. There are five families of bits:
  • Snaffle
  • Pelham
  • Curb
  • Gag
  • Bitless
  All bits can be fitted into one of these categories.

b. There are seven areas where pressure can be applied by various bits:
  • Tongue
  • Bars
  • Lips/corners of mouth
  • Nose
  • Poll
  • Chin groove
  • Roof of mouth

c. A thick mouthpiece will spread pressure over a larger surface area and will therefore be more gentle, while a thin mouthpiece will work in the opposite way and be more severe.

J.A. Allen & Co. Ltd.
The Horseman's Publisher

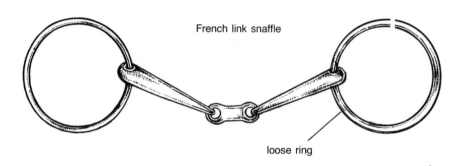

French link snaffle

loose ring

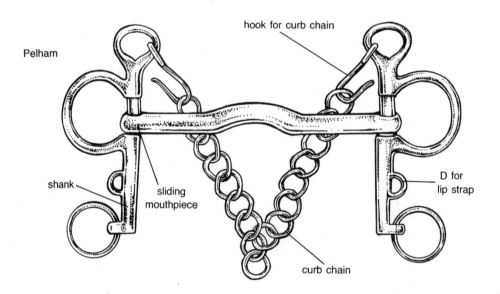

Pelham

hook for curb chain

shank

sliding mouthpiece

D for lip strap

curb chain

Parts of the bit

d. Bits with loose rings or sliding mouthpieces give the bitting arrangement more mobility, while those with fixed mouth-pieces and rings reduce the mobility. The horse's response will vary according to the arrangement used.

e. **Bits with shanks.** The longer the shank above the mouthpiece, the more leverage there is on the poll. The longer the shank below the mouthpiece, the more leverage on the bars.

f. A **snaffle** will apply pressure on the tongue, lips and bars of the horse's mouth.

g. A **curb** bit will apply pressure on the tongue, the bars and the poll.

h. When the snaffle and curb are put together in the form of a **double bridle**, the snaffle has a head-raising action and the curb has a head-lowering action.   (20 minutes)

5. Care of the Equipment

The Thorough Cleaning Process

a. Undo all the buckles and take the tack completely apart. This includes removing stirrups and leathers, girth, numnah, reins, bit, cheekpieces, etc.

b. The bit, stirrups and treads can be washed in warm water, then dried.

c. Remove any jockeys of grease on the leather with a horse-hair pad. This can also be done with a blunt knife if care is taken not to scratch the leather.

d. Using lukewarm water, make a sponge damp, not wet, and work it over all the leather until it is clean.

e. Next, use a damp sponge to apply a layer of saddle soap which should be worked well into the leather.

f. A match stick or tooth pick will make a useful instrument with which to clean all the buckle holes that have become clogged with grease or soap.

g. The stirrups and other metal work can be cleaned with metal polish. Do not apply metal polish to the bit.

h. Girths and numnahs made of washable fabric can usually be hand or machine washed.

i. Synthetic saddles are washed with a stiff brush and lukewarm water, then left to dry.

j. This complete cleaning process should take place after the tack has been used a maximum of five to six times. For horses in regular work, this is usually once a week.

After Each Use

a. Always wash the bit to prevent an accumulation of dried saliva and food, which would soon rub the horse's mouth.

b. Remove the girth and numnah, brush clean and leave to air.

c. If boots are worn, brush or wash clean and leave to air.

d. Slip the bridle straps out of their keepers, and run down the stirrups. With a damp sponge, remove obvious grease, mud and sweat. Work in a layer of saddle soap.

Additional Points on Cleaning and Care

a. While cleaning the tack, keep a constant check on its condition and therefore its safety.

b. If the tack gets very wet, take it apart and leave it to dry. Clean with a damp sponge, then apply a layer of leather dressing. This will replace the oil lost and make the leather more supple. When the dressing has soaked in, apply a layer of saddle soap.

c. New leather will become more supple if leather dressing is applied. All leather will benefit from an application of dressing three or four times a year.

d. Tack should be kept in a warm room. If the atmosphere is damp, the leather will become mouldy and will rot but if it is too warm and dry the leather will dry out and crack.

Checking the Tack for Safety

a. All of the stitching will weaken and rot eventually. At the first signs of weakness, the item concerned should be sent to the saddler for restitching.

b. On the saddle, keep a particularly close check on the stitching that attaches the girth straps to the webbing under the saddle flaps. It undergoes considerable strain and if it rots your girth will no longer be secure!

c. The stitching that secures the buckle of the stirrup leather also takes a lot of strain, as does the stitching on the girth. Check these each time you use them.

d. The girth straps are often stitched to two separate pieces of webbing. If your girth is buckled to the first strap (attached to the first webbing) and either of the second two straps (attached to the second webbing), you have more security should one webbing break. Check the webbing for signs of wear.

e. The vital areas on the bridle include the stitching at the buckle and bit ends of the reins, and on the cheekpieces.

f. Another major area of wear occurs at all the buckle holes. These sometimes stretch so much that one hole begins to run into another. This severely weakens the leather which will then break easily. This frequently occurs on the girth straps.

g. Where straps are always buckled in the same hole, the leather may begin to crack from being constantly bent. (25 minutes)

6. Injuries from Dirty or Ill-fitting Tack

If tack is dirty or does not fit correctly, it will rub, causing galls and bruising. The most common sites of these injuries are:

- The girth area just behind the elbow.
- On top of and on either side of the withers.
- Either side of the spine just under the back of the saddle.
- Behind the ears.
- Just under the projecting cheek bones.
- The corners of the horse's mouth.
- The chin groove.

Treatment

a. Find and remove the cause.
b. Treat as a minor wound.

c. There are various ways in which the horse can be exercised while the wound is healing. Try ride and lead, use a bitless bridle or lunge. (10 minutes)

Follow-up Work

1. Students should practise repeating all the points of the saddle and bridle until they are completely familiar with them.
2. Students should practise fitting saddles, bridles and accessories to a variety of horses.
3. Use question and answer sessions to confirm knowledge:

   a. Name the five families of bits.
   b. To what areas may pressure be applied when using various bits?
   c. Describe how tack is cleaned.
   d. What safety checks should you make before using your tack?
   e. Where would you find a girth gall?

10 Horse Clothing

Time

1 hour 30 minutes

Resources

a. A variety of rugs and rollers, including: day, night, sweat, summer sheet and New Zealand.
b. Blankets.
c. Tail bandages.
d. Stable bandages, Fybagee and gamgee.
e. Travelling boots.
f. Other travelling accessories, including: knee and hock boots, tail guard, poll guard, overreach boots.

Location

The stable yard.

Preparation

a. Tie up the horses in the selected area.
b. Gather equipment and place it within easy reach of the horses. (A mobile saddle horse will be useful here.)
c. Check that the equipment will fit the horses.

Aims

- To teach recognition, use and fit of various items of horse clothing in everyday use.
- To teach how to clean and care for this equipment.

Objectives

- To enable students to fit tack correctly, and thereby prevent injuries/accidents occurring from ill-fitting clothing.
- To improve awareness of safety.

In the stable yard, work through each item of equipment, demonstrating its use, fit and procedure for removal.

1. Rugs

Many different fastenings, materials and designs are used for every possible occasion.

To check your horse's rug size, measure from the middle of its chest right around along its side to the point of its buttock. The rug is measured in a similar way: laid flat on the floor and measured from chest strap to the end of the rug.

To Rug Up

a. When putting the rug on, avoid throwing it over the horse, which may startle it, and aim to keep its hair lying flat. At the same time, take care to fold leg or surcingle straps over the rug to prevent them from swinging against the horse's legs and causing injury.

b. Fold the rug in half, by bringing the tail end forward towards the wither end. Then place the folded rug well forward over the horse's withers. Unfold the rug and slide it back into place. It is best to leave it a little far forward, as it will tend to slip back once the horse begins to move.

c. In general, it is best to fasten the roller or surcingles before the front straps. Some horses bite at the front of their rugs while the roller is being fastened and if the front strap is already buckled the horse could get its lower jaw caught in the front of the rug. Likewise, if the front strap is fastened first on a breezy day, the rug may blow forward and become tangled around the horse's front legs.

d. For the same reasons, undo the front strap first when removing the rug (and leg straps if used).

e. If a roller is used to secure the rug, it needs to be firmly buckled to stop the rug from slipping. To prevent undue pressure there should be plenty of padding between the horse's withers and the roller.

f. Cross-over surcingles incorporated into the rug avoid the pressure problems that rollers can cause and are favoured by many owners. They should be adjusted to hang just 3–5 cm (1–2 in) below the horse's belly. This type of rug is usually darted and shaped to fit the contours of the horse's body more closely. This helps to prevent slipping.

g. As horses are more active in the field, turn out rugs (New Zealands) have leg straps to help to secure them. These should be adjusted to allow freedom of movement and should hang down approximately level with the inner aspect of the second thigh. Fasten one leg strap, then link the other strap through the first one before fastening. The two straps are then linked together, which aids the stability of the rug and prevents rubbing (see page 95).

h. Blankets are less popular now that fitted under-rugs, made from various materials, are available. If a blanket is used, fold it in half and lay it over the horse well forward on its neck. Unfold it and slide it back into place. Take each of the front corners in turn and fold them back towards the withers, leaving a triangular section of blanket pointing forward up the horse's neck. Place the rug on top, then fold the triangular section of blanket back over the top of the rug. It may reach far enough back to be secured under the roller, but this really depends on how large the blanket is. Fasten the rug in the usual way.

i. When removing rugs, undo leg straps, front straps and rollers or surcingles. Fold any trailing straps over the rug then fold the rug in half by bringing the wither end back towards the tail end. Slide the rug back and off, leaving the horse's hair lying flat.

Rugging up using an under blanket

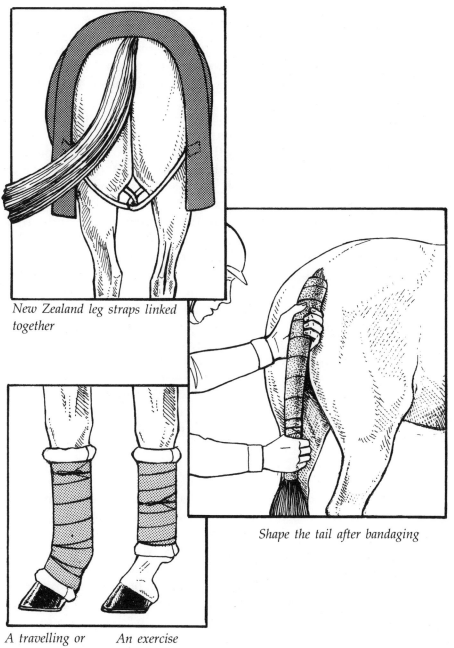

New Zealand leg straps linked together

Shape the tail after bandaging

A travelling or stable bandage

An exercise bandage

Further Points

a. All types of rug should be secured with a roller, surcingle or cross surcingles. This is sometimes forgotten when sweat or summer sheets are used, as they are not always made with surcingles attached.

b. Some turn out rugs are made extra deep at the sides for warmth and protection from the weather.

c. Some rugs may be fitted with a fillet string. This is a piece of cord, attached to the two back corners of the rug, which hangs level with the second thigh and fits around the back of the horse's legs under its tail. The fillet string is used to prevent the back of the rug from blowing out and up in breezy conditions. It is particularly useful on light rugs that may be worn outside at shows or when travelling.

d. Rugs should fit snugly around the base of the horse's neck. If the front section hangs low on the chest, the rug will slip back too easily and rub the horse's shoulders.

   If the length is correct, the rug should reach the top of the horse's tail. If it is much longer or shorter than this, the shaped parts of the rug will not correspond with the shape of the horse.

e. Most rugs will be labelled with washing or cleaning instructions. Those made of washable material may fit in your washing machine, making cleaning easy. (Not all domestic machines are large enough to cope with a large rug.) Waxed or waterproofed rugs will need to be brushed clean and may need rewaxing or reproofing to keep them waterproof. Some companies specialise in rug cleaning and repair. Your saddler will probably know if there is a rug cleaner in your area.

f. How frequently your rugs are washed or cleaned depends entirely upon how much they are worn. A stable rug in constant use will probably need washing every two to four weeks, while a turn out rug may only need cleaning once a year. Any leather work on your rugs should be oiled and saddle soaped as frequently as your other tack.

g. When not in use, rugs should be stored on shelves or hangers in a dry atmosphere. Take precautions against moths and vermin which can easily ruin an expensive rug.

h. Some rugs have woollen linings. These may irritate a horse with sensitive skin, especially if it has been clipped. Other horses may be too warm in a thick quilted rug, or may fit one particular design of rug better than another. All these factors, and others such as cost, need to be considered when choosing a rug.

i. The type of sweat rug that resembles a string vest should always be used in conjunction with a second rug. Used on its own, it has no purpose. The idea is for it to trap a layer of air between the horse and the outer rug. This layer of air circulates and helps to dry a wet horse without letting it become chilled.   (30 minutes)

2. Bandages

Bandages are made in different widths, lengths and materials, for different uses.

Tail Bandage

a. Tail bandages are a little less stretchy than exercise bandages, but are made from a similar material, approximately 7–8 cm (2¾–3 in) wide, with cotton ties.

b. They are used to protect the tail while travelling and to help to improve the horse's appearance by keeping the top of the tail smooth, especially after it has been pulled.

c. A tail bandage should not be left on for more than an hour. As it has to be applied firmly to prevent it from slipping down, it could interfere with circulation if left on too long. This may cause the hair to fall out!

d. Damp the tail hair at the top of the tail before applying the bandage. This aids grip for the first few turns.

e. For even pressure, keep the bandage smooth and overlap each turn evenly, as well as keeping the tension of the tapes, when tied, the same as the bandage.

f. Bandage almost to the end of the dock for a pleasing appearance and a firm base to work around.

g. When travelling, finish the bandage by winding it a few centimetres back up the tail, tie the tapes slightly to one side, and fold the last turn of your bandage down over the tapes to cover them. This helps to prevent them being rubbed undone if the horse leans against its tail in the box. If the bandage is finished and tied too high, the tapes and knot may rub against the horse and cause a sore.

h. Finally, with one hand under the tail, reshape it to follow the contour of the horse's hind quarters, so that the horse is not left with its tail sticking out at an uncomfortable angle (see page 95).

i. To remove the bandage, untie the tapes then slide the whole bandage off in one piece, from the top, down the horse's tail.

Stable/Travelling Bandages

a. Stable/travelling bandages are 10−12 cm (4−4¾ in) in width and made from slightly stretchy material, which may be wool, cotton or synthetic. They may have cotton ties or Velcro fastenings. (See page 95.)

b. They can be used in the stable for warmth, for support after a hard day's competing or to secure a poultice.

c. Used for travelling, they provide support and protection.

d. Fybagee or gamgee is used under these bandages to help distribute even pressure. When travelling, the Fybagee can be cut long enough to extend above and below the bandage to help to protect the coronet bands, knees and hocks.

e. Roll the bandage around the leg in the same direction as the overlap of your Fybagee/gamgee. Otherwise the Fybagee/gamgee will be unrolling as you try to bandage.

Exercise Bandages

a. Exercise bandages are very stretchy, approximately 10 cm (4 in) in width and made from an elastic and cotton mix, with cotton ties. (See page 95.)

b. They can be used to give support when the horse is working. They are most frequently used in cross country or show jumping when brushing boots are less secure.

c. Always use Fybagee/gamgee underneath them.

d. For competition work, it is safer to secure the bandage with tape instead of ties, and to sew the last turn to the rest of the bandage.

Further Points

a. Remove all types of leg bandages by passing the bandage quickly from one hand to the other as you unwind it around the horse's leg. The leg will then benefit from a brisk hand massage to restore normal circulation.

b. Leg bandages can be hand or machine washed as often as necessary. Tapes should be ironed flat after washing, to prevent them from curling up and making pressure ridges when tied around the horse's leg.

c. Gamgee and Fybagee will stand up to gentle hand washing; being stronger, Fybagee will last longer.   (30 minutes)

3. Further Protective Equipment for Travelling

Make sure your horse is familiar with new equipment before the travelling day. For example, hock boots take time to get used to. Use a minimum of equipment for long journeys to avoid sores and discomfort. Choose rugs that are suitable for the weather conditions.

Poll Guard

a. A useful item if there is not much head room in your box or trailer, and if the horse is tall or inclined to resist while being loaded.

b. Some guards only cover the poll, while others extend to protect the eyes and forehead.

c. The poll guard attaches to the head collar. When fitting, check that it will not rub around the ears and that the head collar will not slip back.

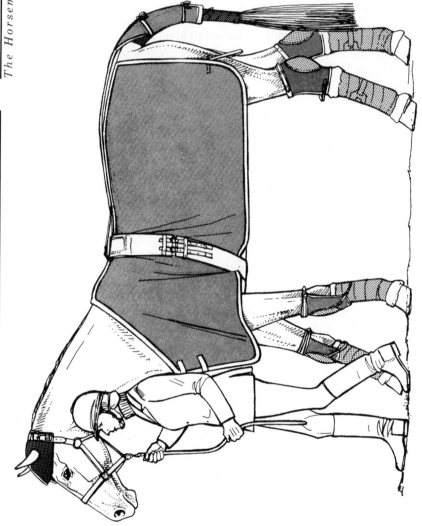

A horse equipped for travelling

Tail Guard

a. This can be put over a tail bandage for short journeys, but should be used on its own for long journeys.
b. This guard protects the very top of the tail. Horses often lean against the trailer ramp for support while travelling, causing this area of the tail to be rubbed raw.
c. Tail guards can be made from wool, cotton, leather or synthetic material, and may fasten with buckles, tapes, zips or Velcro. Attach it to the roller at one end, then position the top of the guard just above the top of the tail, wrap around and fasten.

Knee and Hock Boots

a. The knees and hocks are vulnerable when travelling, as the horse may lose its balance and stumble or knock its joints against the partitions, etc.
b. These boots must be fitted firmly above the knee or hock, to prevent them from slipping down. For this reason they must be well padded around the top strap for comfort.
c. The lower strap needs to be quite loose to allow the joint to flex.
d. Knee boots are also made for exercise purposes, to protect the knees if the horse stumbles on the road. These are called exercise or skeleton knee boots. They consist of a simple knee cap, often with no lower strap and without the extra material found on the travelling type.

Travelling Boots

These come in many different shapes and sizes and are made from a variety of materials. They are a quick and simple alternative to bandages but do not give the same degree of support to tired legs. Most have Velcro fastenings. Some incorporate knee and hock protection.

Overreach Boots

a. Also called bell boots, these are designed to protect the bulbs of the heels from being trodden on from behind, therefore they are used on the front feet only.
b. They are usually made of rubber. Some fasten with buckles, rubber straps or Velcro and others are made to pull on.
c. They are mainly used for exercise but when used in travelling they help to protect the coronet band as well as the heels.
d. The pull on variety can be difficult to get on. Soaking them in warm water for a few minutes will help.

Further Points

a. All equipment should be cleaned regularly. Any leather should be soaped and oiled in the usual way. Boots can be brushed or wiped clean depending on the material. Some can go in the washing machine.   (30 minutes)

Follow-up Work

1. Students should be observed putting on, adjusting to fit, and removing a variety of horse clothing.
2. Question and answer sessions will help to confirm their knowledge:

   a. What equipment should a horse wear for travelling? Explain why.
   b. Why should a tail bandage not be worn on long journeys?
   c. Explain how you would care for the various items of horse clothing used.

11   The Digestive System

Time

1 hour 15 minutes

Resources

a. Handouts.
b. OHP or flip chart.
c. A horse and chalk to draw on it with.
d. Props for mock system; for example, hose pipe, feed sack, football.

Location

The lecture room and the stable yard.

Preparation

a. Copy the correct number of handouts for the students attending.
b. Select a dark-coloured horse that will stand quietly to be drawn on.
c. Select and collect props.
d. Set up the OHP/flip chart in the lecture room.

Aims

- To teach the structure of the digestive system.
- To teach a basic understanding of the system.

Objective

- To increase awareness of the problems when feeding horses and thereby improve feeding management.

Starting in the lecture room, use the OHP or flip chart to illustrate the digestive system while you explain the basic function of each part.

1. Outline and Basic Working of the Digestive System

- Lips – Gather the food.
- Teeth – The **incisors** (at the front) are the cutters. The **molars** (at the back) then grind the food down so that it can be swallowed.
- Tongue – This moves the food from the front to the back and sides of the mouth and then forms a portion of food into a **bolus** ready for swallowing.
- Salivary glands – Saliva is discharged into the mouth through tiny openings. While making the food wet and warm, it also contains enzymes that help to break it down.
- Epiglottis – This blocks the entrance to the **trachea**, to ensure that food only passes down the oesophagus, not into the lungs.
- Oesophagus – Also called the gullet, this is the tube that leads to the stomach. Up to 1.5 m (5 ft) in length, it runs from the throat, down the neck, through the chest between the lungs, then through the diaphragm into the stomach.
- Stomach – This is approximately the size of a rugby ball but expands to accommodate 9–18 litres (2–4½ gal). A muscle called the **cardiac sphincter** controls the inlet into the stomach; another, called the **pyloric sphincter**, controls the outlet. **Gastric juice**, containing enzymes and acid, is added in the stomach, to aid digestion of the food.
- Small intestine – This has three parts. First the **duodenum**, 1 m (39 in) in length; then the **jejunum**, 20 m (66 ft) long; finally, the **ileum**, 2 m (6½ ft) long. All together, these three parts can hold approximately 50 litres (12½ gal). Fluids from

J.A.Allen & Co.Ltd.

The Horseman's Publisher

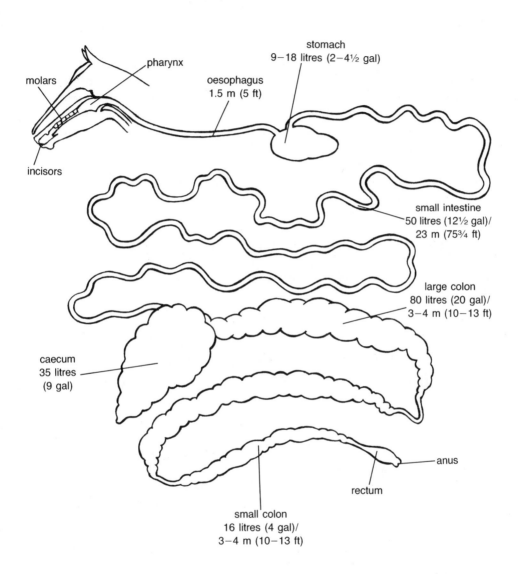

The digestive system

the **liver** and **pancreas** are secreted into the small intestine to break down the food, while some nutrients are absorbed into the blood stream. Muscular contractions, called **peristalsis**, move the food along.

- Large intestine — This starts with the **caecum**, which holds about 35 litres (9 gal) and acts as a holding chamber for the next section, which is called the **large** or **great colon**. The great colon is 3–4 m (10–13 ft) long and holds up to 80 litres (20 gal). From these sections, water is absorbed while bacteria break down the **cellulose** part of the food. This breakdown may take several days. The next section is the **small colon**, where nutrients and water are also extracted. It is 3–4 m (10–13 ft) long, but only holds up to 16 litres (4 gal). It ends in the **rectum**, where the waste material is formed into dung, which then passes out through the **anus**.   (20 minutes)

The students should now have a basic understanding of the system. Move out to the stable yard to use props that will help the students to visualise and remember each section.

2. Practical Lecture, Using Props

a. Using a horse and chalk, point out and draw on the main internal organs. This will help the students to visualise the digestive system in relation to the other organs. Include: heart, lungs, liver, pancreas, stomach, small intestine, ceacum, large colon, kidneys, oesophagus, diaphragm.

b. Use any props available to construct a mock digestive system. Hose pipes, buckets, string, a football — could all be used to give visual meaning to the lengths and capacities mentioned.

    For example, measure out litres of water to show the stomach capacity; measure a length of hose to show how long the small intestines are; and use a feed sack to represent the caecum.   (35 minutes)

Once the students have absorbed the basic outline of the digestive system, some additional information will help to complete the picture.

J.A.Allen & Co.Ltd.
The Horseman's Publisher

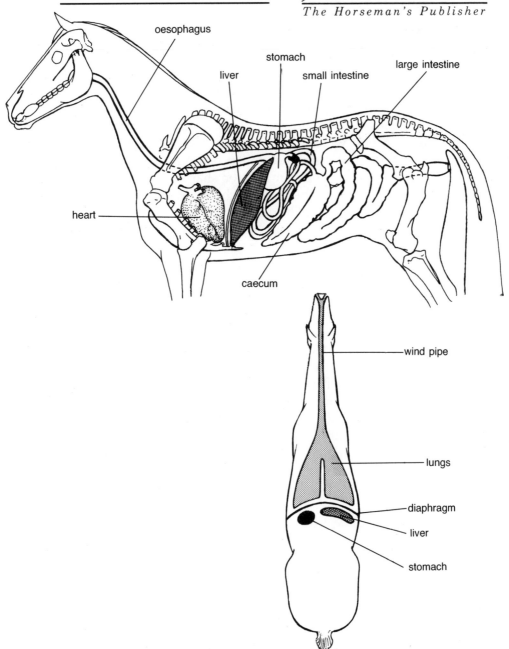

oesophagus

stomach

liver

small intestine

large intestine

heart

caecum

wind pipe

lungs

diaphragm

liver

stomach

The position of the main internal organs

3. Additional Information

a. Teeth — The molars, which are used to grind up the food, wear against each other. As the upper jaw is wider than the lower one, the wear is often uneven. This results in the formation of sharp notches that can cut into the horse's cheeks and tongue. The horse may cease to chew properly, due to discomfort, which in turn may lead to digestive problems, coughing and resistance when being ridden. Taking care not to get nipped, you can feel for sharp edges by slipping your thumb up inside the horse's cheek. Make sure a vet or horse dentist checks your horse's teeth once or twice a year.

b. The digestive tract, from lips to anus, is called the **alimentary canal**.

c. The liver and pancreas are accessory organs that aid digestion. The liver has many functions, one of them being to secrete bile which helps the horse to digest fat. The pancreas secretes digestive juices.

d. The horse's diet contains a large amount of cellulose, which is found in many feeds, especially grass. Cellulose is not broken down until it reaches the large intestine. This means the food passing through the small intestine is still quite bulky.

e. From the food that horses eat, **carbohydrates** are broken down into sugars and used for energy; **fats** and **oils** (**lipids**) are broken down into fatty acids and glycerol; **proteins** are broken down into amino acids and used for body building.

f. It takes approximately 24 hours for the horse to empty a full stomach, but it is better for the stomach to be just half-full most of the time.

g. Food can take three to four days to pass right through the horse.

h. The **cardiac sphincter muscle** acts as a one-way valve which prevents the regurgitation of food.

i. The great colon is so large that it folds back on itself. It also narrows at one of the bends, which makes it prone to blockages.

j. You can see food passing down the oesophagus on the left side of the horse's neck behind the trachea.   (20 minutes)

Follow-up Work

1. Students can practise drawing and labelling the digestive system. This may help them to memorise each part of the structure.
2. They should practise relating each part of the system to the horse itself, so that they can point out, on the horse, the location and approximate size of each internal structure.
3. Question and answer:

   a. What is the alimentary canal?
   b. What accessory organs aid the digestive process?
   c. Where is cellulose digested?
   d. Why do horses need to have their teeth checked?
   e. What does the epiglottis do?
   f. Why are there bacteria in the large intestine?
   g. How long does food take to pass through the horse's system?

12   Feeding

Time

2 hours 10 minutes

Resources

a. A variety of feeding and watering receptacles.
b. Selection of feed stuffs, to include: oats, barley, bran, maize, coarse mix, cubes, sugar beet and hay. (Good and poor samples.)
c. Weighing scales, spring balance and tape measure.
d. Weighbridge.
e. Feed room.
f. Bale of hay and net for weighing.

Location

Lecture room, feed room and stable yard.

Preparation

a. Collect a selection of feed stuffs for use in the lecture room. Include prepared items; for example, soaked sugar beet.
b. Collect feeding and watering receptacles, or note which ones you will observe in the yard.
c. Put hay and haynet in a suitable place for weighing with the spring balance.
d. Check the scales are ready for use in the feed room.
e. If a weighbridge is available, select three or four horses of various height and build, to weigh.

Aims

- To teach recognition of a variety of feed stuffs; to know whether they are of good or poor quality, and how to prepare them.
- To teach the rules of, and a variety of systems for, feeding and watering.
- To teach suitable quantities of feed for horses of various sizes in a variety of work.

Objectives

- To enable students to select suitable types and quantities of feed for a variety of horses in their care.
- To enable students to select suitable systems of feeding and watering for horses in their care.

Start in the lecture room.

1. The Rules of Feeding and Watering

- Feed little and often − This method closely resembles the horse's natural way of feeding. When not stabled, they graze and keep their relatively small stomachs constantly about half-full.
- Only feed good quality feed stuffs − Poor quality feeds can contain mould spores which lead to respiratory disorders and are also low in nutritive value, leading to unthriftiness in the horse.
- Feed at regular intervals daily − Within the daily routine horses soon learn to expect their feeds at certain times. Delay in feeding can lead to frustration and problems such as door banging. At competitions, normal feeding times may need to be adjusted, however the change in routine, new surroundings, etc., should keep the horse occupied, so it may not notice the change in feeding times.
- Only use clean receptacles to hold feed and water − Old food or debris of any sort left in the feed or water bowl, will smell

unpalatable and discourage the horse from eating the fresh food or drinking the water.

- A supply of fresh water must be constantly available — Water is essential for all body functions. Approximately 70% of the adult horse's body weight is water.
- Do not feed directly before exercise — The stomach lies behind the diaphragm. When full, it will press against the diaphragm, restricting expansion of the lungs. At the same time, digestion will slow down as exercise starts. Allow a minimum of one hour after feeding, before exercising.
- Remove water approximately one to two hours before strenuous exercise — For the same reasons as above, too much water in the stomach prior to activities such as racing and eventing, will restrict expansion of the lungs.
- Water before feeding — Although water should be constantly available, the horse will be deprived of it at times; for example, during exercise. Therefore, on return, offer water before feed or the horse may be tempted to eat first, then drink a large quantity of water. This may cause the feed to swell rapidly, as well as diluting the digestive juices and washing feed rapidly through the system, leading to colic or poor digestion.
- Change water buckets a minimum of three times daily — Water left standing in the stable will absorb ammonia. It should be tipped away and replaced with fresh water.
- Do not make any sudden changes to the horse's diet — The horse has bacteria in its large intestine, which help to digest specific feeds. If new feeds are introduced gradually, the bacteria have time to adjust. Sudden changes will upset the bacterial balance, leading to poorly digested feed and colic.
- Feed something succulent daily — Succulent feeds are enjoyed by the horse. When mixed with dry feeds, they improve mastication and digestion.
- Feed plenty of bulk — As the horse's system is designed to digest large amounts, plenty of bulk and roughage are needed to aid digestion of all feeds and keep the system in good working order.
- Give water in small amounts on return from strenuous exercise — After an event or race, when the horse is hot and

breathing heavily, water intake should be restricted. Offer 1–2 litres (2–4 pt) at a time, every 15 to 20 minutes, until the horse has quenched its thirst. It can then be left with a normal water supply. This process prevents large amounts of cold water shocking the system while it is returning to normal.

- Feed according to:
  a. Work being done.
  b. Age.
  c. Time of year.
  d. Whether grass-kept or stabled.
  e. Height and build.
  f. Ability of rider.
  g. Temperament.

All these factors influence the type and quantity of feed. Harder work requires more energy-giving feed, while a laxative diet is needed if the horse is stabled and off work. Youngsters need body-building material; old horses may need softer, cooked foods that are easy to chew and digest. Grass-kept horses need food for warmth in winter, while those stabled can wear extra rugs. Larger horses need more feed than smaller ones, but a large horse with a novice rider should not receive a high-energy diet that may make it difficult to manage. Whatever the size, age, etc., the temperament can vary. You should avoid giving oats to a more excitable type, but may find that a more placid horse does very well on them.   (30 minutes)

2. Feeding and Watering Systems

You may have a variety of feeding and watering systems in your yard and fields, which illustrate the following points. Go out into the yard to observe and discuss them.

Feeding Receptacles

a. Choose a feed bowl that will not constitute a hazard when empty. A horse left with an empty bucket that has a handle can easily catch its leg in the handle and be injured.

Feed mangers suitable for use in the stable

b. Bowls that stand on the floor can be secured within a car tyre. Even if the horse pulls the empty bowl out of the tyre, there are no sharp edges that could cause damage.
c. Mangers that hook over the door work well for some horses. As the design with metal hooks is potentially dangerous, the plastic type is preferable.
d. Mangers that slot into a wall fixing also work well. Check that the fixing has no sharp edges, as many horses remove their mangers when they are empty.
e. Use a manger or feed bowl that can be cleaned easily.

Feeding Hay to Stabled Horses

a. Hay can be fed from the floor. However, it often gets mixed into the horse's bedding, which is wasteful and can encourage the horse to eat its bed.

b. Haynets are useful, making the weighing of quantities easy. When empty, however, they are potentially dangerous as the horse can catch a foot in one and get stuck. They must be tied high off the floor, very securely, be checked frequently and removed as soon as they are empty.

c. Hay racks are another alternative. To prevent the horse from getting its legs caught, the rack must be fixed quite high. This is a drawback, as it means the horse must stretch upwards to eat, causing hay seeds to fall in its eyes and the underline muscles of the neck to become overdeveloped.

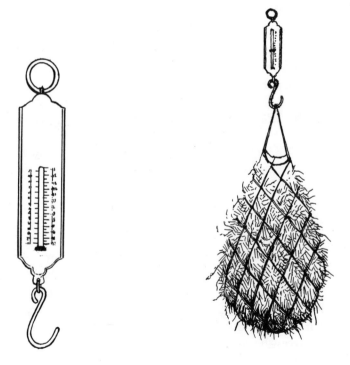

A spring balance for weighing hay in a haynet

Feeding Hay to Field-kept Horses

a. Feeding directly from the ground is the best method. Put out several more piles of hay than the number of horses feeding. In this way, if one horse chases another away, there will always be a spare pile for that horse to move to. To help to prevent poaching, feed the hay in different areas of the field each day.

b. Hay racks are an alternative, but are heavy to move around. Also, if one horse chases another away, that horse may end up with no feed at all.

c. Haynets are dangerous in the field. It would be difficult to tie them high enough for safety, and if one fell down or a horse got its leg caught, it could go unnoticed for some time.

Watering the Field-kept Horse

a. The most basic way of providing water in the field or stable is to use buckets that must be checked and refilled frequently. As mentioned above, however, buckets with handles can be a hazard if knocked over.

b. For several horses in one field, a plastic or iron trough, which can be filled using a hose, is an option. Daily checks will ensure that the trough is clean and full.

c. Self-filling troughs are labour saving but daily checks are just as essential to ensure the trough is working correctly and is full and clean.

d. Troughs and buckets should be situated away from trees and hedges to prevent debris from falling in. They should not be so close to the gate that the entrance becomes blocked when horses gather for water but, if nearby, they will probably be checked more frequently. Troughs should be well clear of the fence to allow the horses free access all round and to prevent kicking and cornering. Alternatively, they can be sited to form part of the fence. This is helpful in adjoining fields, as one trough can supply both at once.

e. A stream may provide an adequate water supply but you need to be sure that it does not come from a polluted source.

Sandy-bottomed streams may result in sand colic as horses are likely to swallow sand when drinking. An approach area of firm standing will be necessary.

f. Access to ponds and any areas of polluted or stagnant water should be fenced off.
g. Troughs and buckets must be checked several times a day in winter to make sure ice is broken.

Watering the Stabled Horse

a. Automatic water drinkers are useful. They provide a constant supply of water in small quantities, which saves wastage and is labour saving. However, it is not always possible to tell how much the horse is drinking. The water bowl must be cleaned out daily and checked frequently to make sure it is not full of hay or bedding. In winter, an alternative method of watering may be required if the system freezes.
b. Buckets, again without handles, work well. They should be secured in a car tyre for stability.   (20 minutes)

3. Types of Feed and Their Preparation

Return to the lecture room and use the feed samples.

Hay — Some General Points

The quality of the hay depends on when it was cut, how quickly it was dried, whether the pasture was free from weeds, and the types of grass.

a. If the hay is cut early, the grass will still be very leafy and moist. A lengthy drying process may cause the leaf to disintegrate and make the hay very dusty. Large amounts of clover in the hay lead to the same problem. If cut too late, the grasses will have gone to seed and lost much of their nutritional value. At the same time, through exposure to wet weather, moulds may have started to form.
b. If dried quickly, the hay will maintain its nutritional value and contain little dust. However, if it rains and the hay is left

J.A.Allen & Co.Ltd.

The Horseman's Publisher

FOR LECTURING PURPOSES

timothy   red fescue   meadow grass   ryegrass

Good grasses to find in permanent pasture and meadow hay

out for several days, mould spores will multiply and the hay will quickly deteriorate and be very dusty.

c. Weeds reduce the feed quality of the hay and can be dangerous. Ragwort, for example, will be readily eaten when dried, but is still poisonous. If it goes unnoticed in the hay ration, it could prove fatal.

d. Good quality grasses give the hay a higher nutritional value.

e. If hay is baled before it is sufficiently dry, it will heat up in the stack and moulds will form.

f. Visibly mouldy hay should not be fed to horses. The tiny mould spores will pass into the horses' lungs, causing inflammation and coughing.

g. The cleanest-looking hay can still carry mould spores. Soaking the hay in clean water will cause the mould spores to swell to a size that prevents them from being inhaled into the lungs, therefore it is advisable to feed soaked hay.

h. Good quality hay smells fresh, tastes sweet, looks clean and when shaken out doesn't appear to be dusty.

i. Poor quality hay will smell mouldy, look grey and dirty, and be very dusty when shaken out. If you can see mouldy patches, it is very poor indeed.

j. Hay is a bulk feed. As the horse's digestive system is designed to digest large amounts of bulk, hay and its alternatives should form a large part of most horses' diets.

Meadow Hay

a. This is made from permanent pasture and contains a variety of grasses.

b. It is the type of hay most frequently fed to horses and is fairly soft and palatable.

Seed Hay

a. This is a crop grown from specially selected seeds. Rye grass is normally used.

b. It is quite a hard hay and more difficult to digest than meadow hay. However, providing it is well made, it has a higher nutritional value and is often used for competition horses.

Threshed Hay

a. This hay is grown from seed in order to produce more seeds that will be sold. It is cut and then threshed to remove the seeds.

b. Good quality grass will be used and, if well made, the hay can be of medium quality. The threshing process will have "battered" the grass and may make it more prone to being dusty.

Haylage

a. This is semi-wilted, vacuum-packed grass.

b. Once the air is excluded, a small amount of fermentation takes place, but moulds do not form. This leaves us with a dust-free alternative to hay.

c. The nutritional value of haylage is higher than that of hay, so smaller quantities are usually fed.

Oats

a. Whole oats may pass through the horse's system undigested, as they have a hard outer layer that the horse has difficulty in digesting. For this reason, oats are usually fed rolled. This process breaks open the oat to expose the nutritious part, the kernel. However, once rolled, the oats will begin to lose their feed value and should be fed within a couple of weeks of purchase.

b. Oats have a thin outer husk that breaks away from the grain. This husk adds fibre to the diet and encourages the horse to chew the oats thoroughly.

c. A good sample should have an equal mix of husk and grain, rather than large amounts of husk. It should be free from dust and any sign of mould. The grain should be clean and fawn-coloured, with a white kernel.

d. Oats are mainly an energy-giving feed and should only be fed to horses in hard work. Some horses become overly excitable when fed oats. For this reason, oats are seldom fed to ponies.

Barley

a. As with oats, barley is usually fed rolled or crushed, to aid digestion.
b. It is also fed boiled. Put the whole grains in water then bring them to the boil and simmer until the grains have swollen and burst open. This makes a warm, tasty, tempting and easily digested feed for a tired horse, especially in winter.
c. There is also cooked, flaked barley, micronised barley and extruded barley. For each different type the manufacturer uses a different cooking process. These processes destroy some of the feed value of the barley but make it easier to digest.
d. A good sample of barley should be similar to oats but there will be no separate outer husk.
e. Barley is mainly an energy-giving feed. It does not tend to make horses as excitable as oats do but it does have a tendency to make them fat.

Maize

a. Whole maize is too hard and indigestible to feed. It is fed in a cooked, flaked form.
b. A good sample will consist of large firm flakes, yellow and white in colour. It should not be dusty, grey nor smell mouldy.
c. Maize is high in energy and inclined to be fattening. It makes some horses overly excitable.

Sugar Beet

a. This product comes in dried and shredded or cubed form and must be soaked before it can be fed to horses. The shreds should be soaked overnight. Fill the selected container half full with shreds then fill almost to the top with cold water. The cubes should be soaked for longer, up to 24 hours, and require more water. Fill the selected receptacle one-third full of cubes and almost to the top with cold water.
b. Sugar beet is high in fibre and provides the horse with a moderate amount of energy. It is a succulent and tasty addition to the diet.

c. A good sample will be sweet-smelling, dark grey in colour and dry without being dusty.

Cubes — (horse and pony/event/stud/complete, etc.)

a. There are many different types of cube, each formulated as a balanced diet for horses and ponies in a particular type of work. Therefore, nutrient levels and energy values will vary.
b. They provide horses with a good balance of nutrients, helping to make sure that nothing is lacking in the diet.
c. A good sample should be dry, so that each cube will break but not crumble.

Coarse Mixes

a. As with cubes, there are many different types, each formulated to provide the right balance of nutrients to horses and ponies in different types of work.
b. The mix often contains molasses, which makes a moist and tasty feed that most horses enjoy.
c. Good samples will be sweet and fresh smelling, with no traces of mould or dust.
d. Like cubes, they provide a good balance of nutrients and are convenient to feed as there is no need to add any other concentrates to the ration.

Chaff

a. This is chopped hay or straw. You may make the chaff yourself, however it can be bought in a molassed form, which is very popular as a tasty addition to the feed.
b. It is added to the concentrate ration to encourage the horse to chew the feed thoroughly. It will help to slow down the type of horse that bolts its feed and also adds fibre to the diet.

Bran

a. This is a byproduct, left over after the milling process of wheat.

b. It is a high-fibre feed and will absorb water easily.

c. It is most useful when made into a bran mash, which can be fed as part of a laxative diet:

> ½–1 kg (1–2 lb) of bran is placed in a bucket. Add boiling water and mix until the consistency is crumbly, not sloppy. Cover with a cloth and leave to cool and steam through. (A teaspoon of salt/handful of oats/Epsom salts, etc., may be added as required.) Feed while still warm.

d. As bran is quite expensive and low in calcium while being high in phosphorous (which is not a good balance for horses), it should only be fed in small quantities, mixed with the rest of the horse's ration.

e. When water is added to dampen the feed, it is absorbed by the bran. This helps to create a moist, palatable mix for the horse. These days, however, mollichaff is often used instead of bran for the reasons given in (d.).

Linseed

a. Linseed is a small, shiny, dark brown seed that comes from the flax plant.

b. It must be cooked before being fed to horses, in order to destroy an enzyme that produces poisonous cyanide.

> Place ½ kg (1 lb) of linseed in a large saucepan. Soak the linseed overnight in approximately 8–10 cm (3–4 in) of water. Bring to the boil and then simmer for several hours. Add more water if necessary, as the seeds will absorb quite a lot during cooking. You should end up with an oily jelly that can be added to the normal feed or to a bran mash.

c. The oil content of the seed helps to add a shine to the horse's coat and generally improves condition.

Succulents

a. The addition of succulents to the diet adds interest, makes the feed more tempting and palatable and provides a useful source of a variety of vitamins.

b. Carrots are most frequently fed and should always be cut

lengthways. Small circles of carrot could become lodged in the oesophagus and cause choking.

c. Apples are usually relished and should be cut into quarters. Do not feed more than two or three at a time.

d. Swedes can be fed whole, left in the horse's manger for it to chew on.   (40 minutes)

4. Deciding What to Feed

Use the feed room, weighing scales, spring balance and haynet, weigh-bridge, and a variety of horses to help to illustrate the following points.

Each horse has very individual requirements. We all know that some humans seem to get fat easily while others always seem to be thin. Also, some are allergic to various foods and others become hyperactive on caffeine or other substances. Horses have similar problems, which means a suitable diet for one horse may not be suitable for another. To formulate a ration, start by following some basic guidelines, then be prepared to alter the diet according to how the horse looks, behaves and performs.

Estimating the Horse's Total Daily Feed Requirement

a. A horse's appetite is equal to approximately 2.5% of its body weight.

b. The ideal way to check the horse's body weight is to weigh it on a weighbridge. If you do not have access to one of these, the weight can be estimated using a weight tape or by referring to a weight chart.

c. Heights and weights for use as an approximate guideline:
    12 h.h. − 230−280 kg (506−616 lb)
    13 h.h. − 280−350 kg (616−770 lb)
    14 h.h. − 350−420 kg (770−924 lb)
    15 h.h. − 420−520 kg (924−1144 lb)
    16 h.h. − 500−600 kg (1100−1320 lb)

d. To work out a daily feed ration for a 16 h.h. horse that weighs 520 kg (1144 lb), divide the body weight by 100 and then multiply by 2.5: 520 ÷ 100 × 2.5 = 13. This figure is the

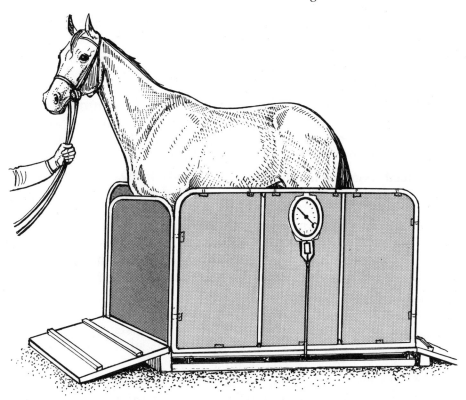

A horse being weighed on a weighbridge

number of kilograms of dry matter that the horse should be fed each day. (1 kg = 2.2 lb.)

e. This total daily feed intake will be split into the horse's hay/haylage/grass ration and its concentrate ration.

    Resting horse − 100% hay/grass ration
    Light work   − 75%   "   "   25% concentrates
    Medium work − 60%   "   "   40%   "
    Hard work   − 40%   "   "   60%   "

f. If the horse on 13 kg (28−30 lb) of feed per day is in medium work, it could have 7.8−8 kg (17−18 lb) of hay and 5−5.2 kg (11−12 lb) of concentrates.   (20 minutes)

Selecting the Right Type of Feed

a. Weigh out the horse's ration rather than giving random scoopfuls. Each scoopful will vary according to whether it is heaped or level.

b. It is always safer to give a horse a low concentrate and high fibre ration. If in doubt, give plenty of soaked hay (weigh the hay ration before soaking) and small amounts of concentrates at first. If the horse is well behaved, looking well, working well and happy in itself, then there is no need to alter this balance of feed.

c. If it is too energetic and silly, the concentrate ration should be cut down and more hay given. If it is lethargic and struggling to do the work asked, despite a progressive fitness programme, it probably needs more concentrate and less hay.

d. Use low-energy feeds for horses in light work; for example horse and pony nuts, non-heating coarse mix, sugar beet.

e. Give sick and resting horses a laxative diet of sugar beet and chaff, or bran mashes, and plenty of soaked hay.

f. Old horses need easily digested feeds such as micronised or boiled barley, or coarse mix.

g. Horses with respiratory problems may need haylage rather than soaked hay. As haylage is very nutritious, the concentrate ration may have to be cut back to avoid the horse receiving overly large amounts of high-energy feed.

h. If your horse tends to bolt its feed, place a salt or mineral block in its manger. Having to eat around this will slow it down. It will also have the salt and minerals available to lick as required. A whole swede could be used for this purpose too.

i. For those owners with one or two horses, a coarse mix or cubes and chaff will eliminate the need to buy several bags of different feeds, which can lead to waste.

j. Larger yards may buy oats, barley, cubes, sugar beet and chaff to cater for the needs of a wider variety of horses in different work.

k. As work is gradually increased during a fitness programme, the concentrates should also be increased while the hay ration is decreased. All changes must be made gradually.

l. As the concentrate ration is increased, it should be divided into several small feeds. Three to four feeds a day usually fit well into the work routine.

m. Having decided on a feed ration, make a chart in the feed room and write up the quantities and types of feed to be given to each horse. This will ensure that the horse's diet is not changed suddenly if different people feed the horse from time to time. Keep the feed chart up to date.   (20 minutes)

Follow-up Work

1. Students should be tested in their ability to recognise different feed stuffs and to describe the quality and basic value of each feed.
2. To gain experience in formulating rations and quantities, students should practise weighing out hay and concentrate rations for a variety of horses in different work.
3. Practice should be given in preparing feeds such as boiled barley, sugar beet, linseed and bran mashes.
4. Question and answer:

    a. Give three rules of feeding and explain why we should follow these rules.
    b. What factors will influence the quality of a hay crop?
    c. What do you look for in a good sample of hay?
    d. What do you consider is a safe method of feeding hay/concentrates to stabled/grass-kept horses?
    e. How do you decide how much feed to give your horse each day?
    f. What would you feed a 15 h.h., 450-kg (990 lb) horse in light work?
    g. What factors influence what you feed each horse?
    h. Does the horse's temperament influence what you feed it?
    i. How do you divide the total daily feed ration at the beginning and end of a fitness programme?

13 Fitness Work: Preparation and Roughing Off

Time

1 hour 30 minutes

Resources

a. A selection of horses known to the students, at different levels of fitness.

Location

Lecture room.

Preparation

a. Make notes about the fitness levels of selected horses; for example, what they are being prepared for, if on holiday and why, ailments or injuries.

Aims

- To teach the students how to prepare an unfit horse for work, with due regard for its health and well being.
- To teach how to let the horse down again for a rest period.

Objective

- To help students to understand how to keep their horses healthy and sound in wind and limb while working them at their required level.

Start off in the lecture room.

1. Bringing a Horse up from Grass/Rest

An event horse will usually have a winter break and a hunter a summer break. An injured horse will be forced to rest during the healing of the injury and some horses may simply have a break when their owners go on holiday.

The time of year and type of rest period will influence the procedure to be followed in order to prepare the horse for work again. A summer holiday at grass means the horse is likely to be a little overweight and in soft condition. However, its muscles, tendons and ligaments will be firmer than those of a horse that has been confined to box rest because of injury.

Horses on winter holidays will have been given concentrate feeds and hay to make up for a lack of grazing, while horses on summer grazing will have to be reintroduced to this type of feed.

a. Prior to starting the fitness programme, arrange for the vet to give any vaccinations due; for example, 'flu and tetanus. He or she can also recommend what type of wormer you should dose your horse with at this stage.

b. Either the vet or a horse dentist should check the horse's teeth.

c. Contact the farrier and have the horse shod. Stud holes may be needed from the beginning so that road studs can be used.

d. Order feed, hay/Haylage and bedding.

e. Check that your stables are clean and in good repair.

f. Check that all your tack, rugs and accessories are clean, repaired where necessary and ready to use.

g. The horse that has been at grass should be brought into its stable for a short period each day. This will help it to adjust to standing in again. It can gradually be kept in for longer and longer periods. As it has been in a fresh outdoor environment, take care to keep the stable well ventilated and free from dust in order to avoid respiratory problems.

h. While standing in, the horse can also gradually be reintroduced to concentrate feed and hay. Start with small amounts, damp the feed and soak the hay.

i. Horses on winter holidays will probably have been stabled at night and are therefore already accustomed to the aforementioned points (g.) and (h.).

j. Begin grooming, as it will take some time to clean all the grease from the coat, especially if the horse has a winter coat, which you will need to clip in a few weeks' time. Do not clip until the horse has completed one or two weeks of its fitness programme. It will need its coat to keep it warm while it is only at the walking stage.

k. The mane and tail can gradually be pulled and the feathers trimmed.

l. Rub surgical spirit into areas of soft skin that need to be hardened ready to take the girth, saddle and bridle.

m. Introduce light rugs. This will help to improve the coat if you are coming into the summer months, and will prepare the horse for heavier rugs if you are heading for winter.

n. Finally, if you are hunting or competing, make sure you have paid your subscription, membership or entry fees.

(20 minutes)

2. The Fitness Programme

Refer to the selected horses where possible, in order to illustrate any of the following points.

a. With the horse in a correct outline, steady and purposeful walking on firm ground will "tone up" muscles, tendons and ligaments, making them strong and ready for the work to follow. As work progresses, the efficiency of the heart and lungs will gradually improve.

b. Horses that are recovering from injury need a slow beginning to their fitness programme, with many weeks of walking. If recovering from tendon/ligament injury, they may need anything from four to eight weeks or even more, depending on the severity of the injury. Your vet will advise you.

c. Mature, experienced horses will need one to two weeks of walking. Start with half an hour and increase the time each day until you are walking for one to one and a half hours.

d. Always be aware of the type of ground you are working on. Soft, deep going will pull and strain tendons/muscles, especially when the horse is still in soft condition. A horse is also likely to overreach when its feet are held by deep mud.

e. Only walk, or trot very gently, for short periods when on hard ground and roads. The concussion created when the horse's hooves meet the hard ground can lead to strain and inflammation. Roads are also very slippery, which means that trotting can be dangerous.

f. Stony ground can cause bruised soles and uneven ground may cause a slip or trip, leading to strains.

g. Although lungeing is a strenuous activity, generally used when the horse is fairly fit, it may be necessary to lunge a very fresh horse before you ride it. Some horses take time to settle into the working routine. If they are inclined to buck and generally misbehave, it will be safer to lunge for 10−15 minutes first.

h. Continue to turn your horse out whenever possible. Providing it does not have access to large amounts of grass, is not inclined to pace the fence line or gallop about and appears content, it will benefit from the fresh air and space to move. Horses confined to the stable for 20 or more hours a day, are likely to stiffen up, suffer from circulatory problems and develop stable vices.

i. The best way to increase fitness, without increasing concussion, is to introduce hill work. Start with gentle slopes, then gradually work up steeper and longer hills each day. Providing the horse is kept in a good outline, it will really have to use its topline muscles. Also, the greater effort required for walking or trotting uphill will make the horse physically stronger while developing the efficiency of its heart and lungs.

j. Each rider's routine will vary according to where they live. Some may have to cover many miles of road to reach good riding country, while others may have easy access to woodland, hills, etc. It may be necessary to travel by horse box to a good area for cantering or hill work. This can be good practice for younger horses, teaching them to enjoy travelling and remain relaxed.

k. Throughout the programme, observe your horse's respiratory rate, making sure its breathing quickly returns to normal after

Always work the horse in a good outline when riding out. Hill work is particularly beneficial

any period of work. If not, you are doing too much work too soon. Check the horse's legs, which should be cool, firm and free from swelling. Any deviation from normal may indicate that you have progressed to fast work too quickly, or that you are overfeeding concentrate feed.

l. All being well, introduce trotting into your daily programme. Start with approximately one minute, preferably on a gentle upward slope. Include two to four short trots spaced out over the one to one and a half hours' work. Each day, the length of time spent in trot can be gradually increased. Again, avoid concussion by using slopes and hills where possible.

m. In the early stages of the programme, some riders will not give their horse a day off. They may just ride it gently for a short period so that it has an easier day. This routine is helpful if you have limited turning out facilities, however most riders work their horses for six days a week and give one complete rest day.

n. Once the trotting phase has been well established over a period of two to three weeks, canter work can be introduced in exactly the same way. Keep the canter steady, with the horse working in a good outline.

o. Always make sure the horse is well warmed up before trotting or cantering. Purposeful walk for at least a quarter of an hour is essential for loosening and warming up the muscles, especially if the horse has come straight out of the stable.

p. Either just before, or just after, canter work has been introduced, work in the school can be included. Excitable horses may be calmer about having their first short canter in the school rather than out in the woods.

q. Start with 15–20 minutes' school work, using mainly walk and trot, and keeping to large circles and simple movements. Gradually increase the school work according to your horse's needs. (An event horse will need more than a hunter, for example.) Some horses will work and concentrate better if you go straight into the school work before hacking out to do your fitness work. Most horses will benefit from the warming and loosening-up effect of the fitness work, prior to going into the school.

r. At this stage you may start to split the work up into two sessions. The horse may be working from one to two and a half hours a day, depending upon the type of work done. More intensive work in the school will result in a shorter working session, while steady walk and trot work will mean longer sessions.

s. Introduce show jumping and cross country practice as necessary once you have built up the schooling over a period of one or two weeks.

t. In general, a week's work will follow a pattern that includes a regular rest day, schooling and jumping once or twice a week and basic fitness work on the days between. Some horses will benefit from a short schooling session every day.

u. In the last two to three weeks of the programme, those horses that will be doing fast work (hunters, eventers, etc.) will need to do some more purposeful canter work, followed by a "pipe opener". Select a suitable stretch or field where you can canter steadily for two to three minutes, then gently move the horse on to approximately half a minute of gallop, followed by gradually returning to walk. Never pull up quickly and always finish with a long period of walk while the horse gradually recovers its normal respiratory rate. If your build-up work has been correct, it should recover within two to five minutes.

v. An experienced hunter will need a six- to eight-week programme. Cub hunting will then help to prepare the horse for a full day's fox hunting. A novice event horse will need 10–12 weeks to prepare for its first novice event, and a more advanced event horse will need approximately 16 weeks.

w. The ratio of concentrate to bulk feed will gradually change during the programme. Start with approximately 70% bulk and 30% concentrate. Each week the bulk can be lowered and the concentrate increased, until you finish up with approximately 40% bulk and 60% concentrate.   (30 minutes)

3. Associated Ailments

Ailments most commonly associated with fitness work include:

- Respiratory problems brought about by being stabled in a poorly ventilated environment, and by being fed hay contaminated with mould spores.
- Strains to muscles, tendons and ligaments due to working an unfit horse too hard too quickly.
- Bruised soles from trotting or cantering over uneven and stony ground.
- Galls caused by tack that may be dirty or ill fitting rubbing against soft skin.
- Overreach wounds caused by the horse working in an unbalanced manner or moving too fast through deep going.
- Bruising and inflammation from the effects of concussion, brought about by working too fast on roads and very hard ground.

All of the above can be avoided through good management and progressive ridden work. The unavoidable does happen, however. For example, a setback may be caused by the horse treading on a stone while out in the field, resulting in a bruised sole. The fitness programme may then need to be extended by one or two weeks. Allow for this when planning your first competition. Count back the required number of weeks from the competition date to the start of the fitness programme, then go back one or two more weeks to allow for injury. (10 minutes)

4. Care After Hard Work

On return from hunting, eventing or other strenuous activity, the horse will need special attention. It needs to be made comfortable so that it can rest while its systems return to normal. At the same time, being tired, it will benefit from the minimum of fuss.

a. Try to return home with a cool, dry horse. If it is wet, warm and sweaty, it will need to be walked in hand until dry and cool. Some stables may be equipped with infra-red lamps for drying horses. Whichever method is used, the first priority is to get the horse dry but not to allow it to become chilled.

b. In some areas of the country horses return from hunting so caked in mud and clay that the only solution is to bath them immediately. A supply of warm water, shampoo and a washing-down area out of the wind are required. The bathing/ rinsing process should be quick and thorough. Again, the first priority is to keep the horse warm and get it dry as quickly as possible.

c. The horse may be thirsty but should not be allowed to drink large amounts of cold water. Add a small amount of hot water to a bucket of cold water. (Just enough to take the chill off.) Offer water to the horse every 15–20 minutes, allowing it to drink 2 or 3 litres (4 or 6 pt) at a time. Once it has quenched its thirst, it can be left with a normal supply of water.

d. Any obvious wounds should have been noticed and dealt with accordingly. The horse now needs to be carefully checked for any hidden cuts, bruises or swellings. Early discovery and attention will aid a quick recovery.

e. The horse should have a deep, warm bed and be rugged with light warm rugs suitable for the time of year. A tired horse will often feel the cold more. Stable bandages will keep its extremities warm, at the same time giving support to tired limbs.

f. If the horse was not bathed, a light grooming will remove enough dried mud and dried sweat to make it comfortable. Always pick out the feet.

g. Feed the usual hay ration and also a light, easily digested concentrate feed. A bran mash with linseed would be warming and enjoyable.

h. Having settled the horse, return at intervals to check its behaviour. Some horses break out in a secondary sweat and will need to be walked and dried again. Others may suffer a colic attack. Hourly checks should be sufficient unless you suspect a problem, in which case check every 15–20 minutes.

i. The following day the horse may be stiff or even lame. It should be led out in hand to help it to loosen up. Then trot it up to check for soundness. All being well, it will benefit from a day in the field, where it can rest but also gently exercise its tired muscles.   (15 minutes)

5. Roughing Off

After a season of hard work, most horses will need a rest. This may be a complete rest, turned out to grass 24 hours a day, or a period of gentle activity, perhaps partly stabled and ridden out for an enjoyable hack most days.

a. Begin by reducing the concentrate ration and increasing the bulk.

b. Reduce the amount of exercise gradually. (Stop schooling, jumping and fast work straightaway.)

c. If the horse is having a winter break in the field, allow its coat, mane and tail to grow for warmth and protection. (It may need a New Zealand rug.) Also groom less so that grease returns to the coat to make it waterproof.

d. Reduce the number or thickness of rugs worn. This will encourage the coat to grow.

e. Begin turning the horse out in the field for longer periods. This process should be gradual if it has not had access to much grass and is now going to have a summer holiday.

f. If vaccinations, worming or tooth rasping are due soon, now is a good time.

g. If the horse is not going to be ridden, you may have all or just the hind shoes removed.

h. For those horses that will be staying out at night, pick the best possible weather for their first night out.

i. If the horse has not been turned out daily during its working season, it is likely to be very excitable when first let loose. Ride it first to make it a little tired, put brushing boots on all four legs for protection and turn it out hungry so that it is keen to settle and eat the grass.

j. This whole process will take approximately two weeks.

(15 minutes)

Follow-up Work

1. Where possible, students should gain first-hand experience, with guidance, of getting a horse fit for a particular type of work. This should include planning the programme and all the preparation work.

2. Students need to observe the respiratory rates of fit and unfit horses at work in order to become familiar with what to expect and aim for. This also applies to observation of the lower limbs and general muscle development.

3. Question and answer:

    a. What preparation is needed prior to starting a fitness programme?

    b. How might preparation vary at different times of year?

    c. Why is walking exercise so important?

    d. How will you introduce trot work?

    e. How will you alter the horse's diet as its fitness improves?

    f. What ailments can be avoided through good management and riding during the programme?

    g. How will you care for a horse that has just returned from a long day's hunting?

    h. Explain how you will go about "roughing off" your horse.

    i. How will the "roughing off" routine vary at different times of the year?

14 The Foot and Shoeing

Time

1 hour 35 minutes

Resources

a. A horse or pony that will tolerate having aspects of the shoeing process demonstrated on it.
b. A selection of horses with shoeing and foot growth at different stages of wear.
c. A complete set of farrier's tools.
d. A standard hunter-type shoe.
e. Handouts.

Location

Lecture room first, then the stable yard, in an enclosed area for safety.

Preparation

a. Copy the correct number of handouts for the students attending.
b. Lay out the farrier's tools and hunter shoe in the yard area selected.
c. Check that the horse has clean feet and legs and have a headcollar ready to tie it up outside.

Aims

- To teach the students the basic process when shoeing horses.
- To teach how to recognise when the horse needs reshoeing.

Objective

- To help students to understand how the farrier keeps the horse's feet in good form, and how the horse's owner can help to keep the horse's feet in good condition.

Start off in the lecture room.

1. The Structure of the Foot

a. The foot is designed to support the horse, reduce concussion, resist wear and provide grip.
b. Because we demand more from the horse than nature intended, the foot often needs protection to prevent it from wearing down more quickly than it can regrow. By shoeing it, the foot is protected and extra grip is provided.
c. Shoeing can also be used to correct faults and heal ailments and injuries.

The External Structure

- The outer wall of the hoof is hard and insensitive. Divided into toe, quarters and heels, it doesn't quite form a circle because it turns inwards at the heels to form the **bars**. This allows for expansion and provides extra strength at the heels. The wall is made of **horn** which contains many **tubules** that grow down from the top to the bottom of the wall.
- The **coronet** band forms the junction between the lower limb and the wall.
- From just above the coronet grows the **periople**. This is a thin layer of skin that grows down over the wall and controls evaporation of moisture from the horn.
- Most of the ground surface of the foot consists of the **sole** which is concave to the ground.
- The **white line** can be seen between the edge of the sole and the wall. This is the visible part of the **horny laminae**.
- The area of sole between the wall and the bars is called the **seat of corn**.

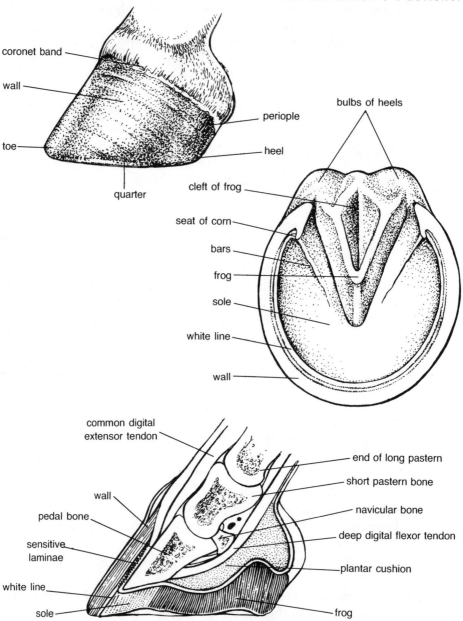

coronet band

wall

toe

quarter

periople

heel

bulbs of heels

cleft of frog

seat of corn

bars

frog

sole

white line

wall

common digital
extensor tendon

wall

pedal bone

sensitive
laminae

white line

sole

end of long pastern

short pastern bone

navicular bone

deep digital flexor tendon

plantar cushion

frog

The structure of the foot

- The rest of the ground surface is occupied by the **frog**. This is wedge-shaped, formed from soft, elastic horn and has a central cleft. It aids grip and helps to absorb concussion.
- At the rear of the hoof are the **bulbs** of the heels.

The Internal Structure

- The inner aspect of the wall is lined with the **horny laminae**, then the **sensitive laminae**, which interlock with the **pedal bone** and help to support it within the foot.
- Above the sole is the **sensitive sole**.
- The bones within the foot consist of the **pedal bone**, the **navicular bone** and part of the **short pastern bone**.
- The **deep flexor tendon** of the lower limb passes into the foot, under the navicular bone and attaches to the pedal bone. The **common digital extensor tendon** of the lower limb passes into the foot, over the short pastern bone and attaches to the pedal bone.
- Above the frog is the **plantar cushion**
- These sensitive, internal structures are supplied with blood through many capillaries. They also help the horse to feel and sense what it is walking on.
- Around the sides of the foot are the **lateral cartilages**, which merge with the bulbs of the heels.
- Being elastic, the frog, bars, plantar cushion and lateral cartilages all help to absorb concussion and disperse it upwards and outwards. (20 minutes)

2. The Shoeing Process and Farrier's Tools

In the stable yard.

To train as a farrier is a long and expensive process. As a result there is a shortage of good reliable farriers. It will be to your advantage to help your farrier to do a good job.

(Each time a different tool is mentioned, identify that tool and demonstrate how it might be used without actually using it on the foot or shoe. Allow the students to handle and become familiar with each

J.A. Allen & Co. Ltd.
The Horseman's Publisher

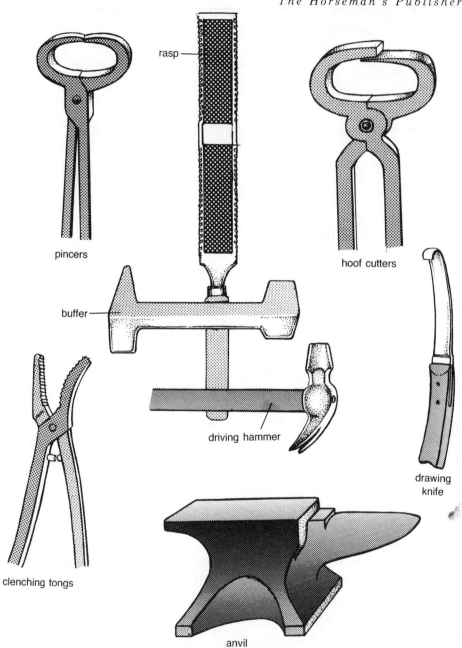

rasp

pincers

hoof cutters

buffer

driving hammer

drawing
knife

clenching tongs

anvil

Shoeing tools

item. Ideally, this part of the lecture should be given while observing the farrier at work.)

 a. Let your farrier know in advance if your horse requires any special type of shoes, or if it is a youngster being shod for the first time.
 b. Horses being shod for the first time should be used to having their feet picked out and be familiar with having the wall and sole of the foot tapped, to prepare them for the nailing-on process.
 c. You should always present horses for shoeing with clean, dry feet and legs.
 d. Provide the farrier with a well-lit area and dry, hard standing, if possible undercover.
 e. The first time the farrier shoes your horse, he should find out about its way of going and, assuming the horse is already shod, he should look at the wear of its shoes and the growth of its feet. With your help, he will then be able to determine whether the horse has any problems, such as overreaching, stumbling, dragging its toes, etc. With problems such as these, he may choose a different type of shoe.
 f. If the farrier is hot shoeing, he will have brought a mobile **forge** in which to heat the shoes. Using **fire tongs**, he will place the selected shoes in the forge, to heat them ready for use.
 g. Next, he will remove the old shoes. The **buffer, driving hammer** and **pincers** will be used for this process. The flat end of the buffer is placed under the clench. When hit with the hammer the buffer eases under the clench to lever it up. When all the clenches have been "knocked up", the pincers are used to lever off the shoe, working from the heel towards the toe. Care is taken not to break off any chunks of horn. A front foot may be supported between the knees, to leave the hands free to hold and use the tools. The farrier's apron provides protection and comfort at this stage. A hind foot will not be held in this way, as the horse could kick out and knock the farrier over!
 h. Depending on how much growth of foot there is, the **hoof cutters, drawing knife** and **toeing knife** will now be used to

J.A.Allen & Co.Ltd.
The Horseman's Publisher

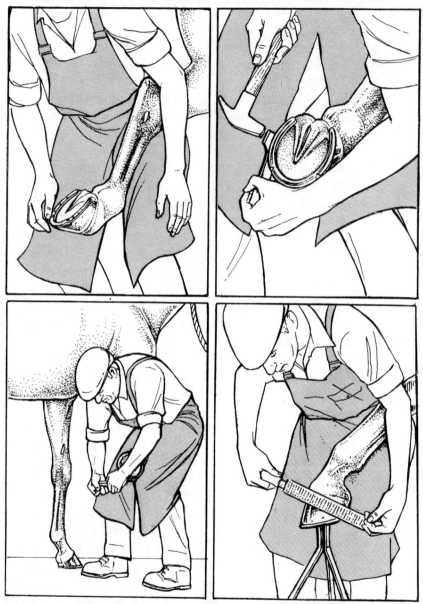

Holding the foot — the hind foot is supported on the farrier's leg, leaving his hands free to use the tools; the front foot is supported on the tripod or between the farrier's knees, again leaving his hands free

remove excess growth of horn. (Make sure the students can see the difference between the hoof cutters and the pincers.)

i. The **rasp** will now be used to level off the surface to which the shoe will be applied. The rasp or the drawing knife is used to make a notch for the toe clip.

j. One of the hot shoes will now be removed from the forge with the fire tongs. It will be placed on the **anvil** and the **pritchel** will be knocked into one of the nail holes to enable the farrier to carry the hot shoe to the horse.

k. Using the pritchel, the farrier will put the hot shoe firmly into place on the foot so that it burns into the insensitive horn. This process allows the farrier to see if he has prepared the foot correctly and shaped the shoe to fit as perfectly as possible.

l. He will make adjustments, where necessary, by taking the shoe back to the anvil. While holding the shoe with the shoe tongs, he will hammer it into shape with the **turning hammer**, often returning it to the forge to be reheated. He may also further improve the shape and levelness of the foot with the rasp.

m. Once he is completely happy with the fit of the shoe, he will cool the shoe in a bucket of water and prepare to nail it on.

n. In order to make sure that the shoe is nailed evenly in place, the farrier will hammer in the nails by alternating from side to side, usually starting at the toe. Once the nail is driven in, the claw end of the driving hammer is used to twist off the sharp end of the nail.

o. The blunt end of the nails, left after the sharp points have been twisted off, will now be knocked down to form the clenches. The farrier will place the horse's foot on the **tripod** and use the rasp to make a "bed" in the wall of the foot to knock the clenches into. The **clenching tongs** will be used to pull the clenches down tightly. The farrier may also hammer down the clenches.

p. The whole process will be finished off with the rasp, which will be used to smooth off any ragged bits of horn that may be overlapping the shoe. A well-shod foot should appear flush with the shoe all the way round and the clenches should be fairly level, approximately a third of the way up the wall.

At the toe the wall of the foot should slope at an angle of approximately 45 degrees in the front feet and 50 degrees in the hind feet.   (35 minutes)

3. Parts of the Shoe

- Toe clip/quarter clips − These help to keep the shoe in place on the horse's foot and prevent it from slipping backwards or sideways.
- The fuller − This is the groove in which the nail heads sit. This helps to prevent the nail heads from wearing away too quickly and also aids grip.
- The ground-bearing/foot-bearing surfaces
- Pencilled heels − Help to prevent the heels of the shoe from being trodden on from behind and therefore help to prevent the shoe being pulled off.
- The nail holes − Usually four on the outside branch of the shoe and three on the inside branch. The farrier will generally use only as many nails as are necessary to keep the shoe in place. Smaller ponies will have fewer nails.
- Concave slope − This slope makes the shoe concave to the ground, thereby helping to prevent the shoe from being sucked off in heavy going.   (10 minutes)

4. Recognising the Need for Reshoeing

Most horses need reshoeing every four to six weeks. This will depend upon how much road/hard ground work the horse does, how quickly the hoof grows and whether the shoe becomes twisted, loose, lost, etc. If available, use a variety of horses to show the following:

- Part or all of the shoe has worn thin, resulting in less grip. This can be dangerous, especially when riding on the road.
- A loose shoe − It may twist off at any time. The cast shoe may then be trodden on by the horse, causing a nail to puncture its sole.

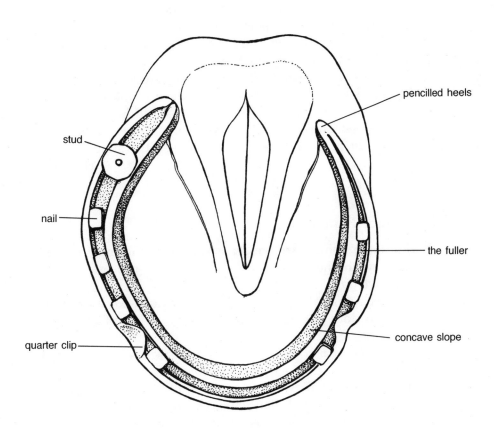

stud

nail

quarter clip

pencilled heels

the fuller

concave slope

The parts of the shoe

- Risen clenches — The shoe will soon be loose and a risen clench can cause damage if the horse brushes.
- Long feet — If the foot looks long at the toe, pick it up and examine the heel area. Excess growth will have moved the shoe forward, causing the foot to grow over the shoe at the heels. This can push the heels of the shoe onto the seat of corn, resulting in bruising and lameness.
- The horse may have cast a shoe. In this case check that all the nails have been removed from the wall.
- Twisted shoe — Due to the shoe being trodden on by another horse, or by the horse treading on a front shoe with a hind foot, it may be twisted. This could lead to lameness.
- Cracked and broken feet — Horses with brittle feet may lose chunks of horn. This is likely to loosen the shoe.

(15 minutes)

Further Points

1. If a horse's shoes are hardly worn, the farrier may reshoe the horse with the same set of shoes. This process is called a "remove".
2. Cold shoeing takes place if the farrier does not have a mobile forge. It does not quite equal the close, precise fit achieved by hot shoeing.
3. If you live near to the farrier's work base, you may hack your horse to him, rather than have him travelling to you.
4. It takes a day or two for the horn of the hoof to bed down around the newly driven nails. During this period the shoe is less secure, therefore it is unwise to ride your horse at faster paces or through mud for the first day or two, or you may find the new shoes are lost.
5. The rasping process will remove some of the periople from the wall of the foot. Hoof oil will help to protect the foot while the periople grows over the wall again.
6. The pritchel end of the buffer may be used for cleaning out nail holes; for example, when a used shoe is being reused and an old nail head may need removing.

7. The cost of a set of shoes will depend upon various factors: type and size of shoes/stud holes/special shoes, and so on.
8. The foot wall grows at the rate of approximately 1–1½ cm per month. The growth rate may accelerate; for example, if the horse has access to spring grass. Irregular rates of growth can be seen as "grass rings" on the wall of the hoof.
9. Only attempt to remove a shoe yourself if it has slipped badly to one side and is in danger of harming the horse or if more damage will be done to the foot by leaving it. It is better to wait for the farrier. In the UK it is illegal for anyone who is not a registered farrier to put a shoe on a horse.

(15 minutes)

Follow-up Work

1. Students should watch a farrier at work and see the whole shoeing process. The supervising instructor can ask the students to:

   a. Name each tool as it is used.
   b. Say what the farrier is likely to do next.

2. Students should practise simulating the process of removing a shoe. They need to be able to hold a front or hind foot while correctly handling the tools needed for shoe removal.
3. Students need practice in assessing a well-shod foot and a foot that needs reshoeing.
4. Question and answer:

   c. In what part or parts of the shoeing process is the pritchel used? (Substitute each of the shoeing tools in turn in this question.)
   d. How should you prepare the horse for the farrier's visit?
   e. Is there any information you should give the farrier before he visits?
   f. If your horse has a "remove", what does this mean?
   g. Point out the following on the horse's shoe: toe/quarter clips, the fuller, the ground/foot-bearing surfaces, pencilled heels.

15 The Smart Horse and Loading and Unloading

Time

2 hours 10 minutes

Resources

a. A horse that needs trimming.
b. A horse with mane and tail suitable for plaiting.
c. Scissors, comb, plaiting needle, bands and thread.
d. Body brush and stencil for quarter markings.
e. A well-behaved horse that will load into a trailer or horse box.
f. Loading aids; for example, lunge lines, bowl of feed.
g. Horse box and trailer ready for loading.

Location

Stable yard.

Preparation

a. Tie up selected horses in an enclosed area.
b. Collect equipment for plaiting, trimming, etc.
c. Put protective clothing on the horse to be loaded.
d. Park the horse box and trailer in safe locations for loading practice.
e. Put loading aids by the trailer.

Aims

- To teach the students how to improve the horse's appearance.
- To teach the students safe procedure for loading and unloading horses into and out of horse boxes and trailers.

Objectives

- To promote high standards of stable management and presentation.
- To improve the understanding of safety and awareness of the horse's needs and reactions.

1. Trimming

Using the selected horse, demonstrate how each area is trimmed.

a. Use blunt- and curved-ended scissors for trimming, to help to prevent injury to the horse.
b. Many horses have long tufts of hair sprouting from their ears. The hair inside the ears is needed to protect the inner ear from entry by foreign particles but the longer tufts that stick out can be trimmed. Gently close the edges of the ear together, then trim away the long hair that is still protruding, cutting it level with the edges of the ear.
c. Make a bridle path by cutting away approximately a 3-cm (1½ in) section of mane just behind the ears where the bridle headpiece will sit. Use a comb to make a neat parting between mane and forelock prior to cutting.
d. Some horses grow long hair under the lower jaw, resembling a beard. This can be trimmed close to the jaw bone.
e. Some owners like to trim away the long whiskers that grow around the muzzle area. These whiskers are part of the horse's sensory equipment and I prefer to leave them untrimmed.
f. About 8−10 cm (3−4 in) of mane over the withers may be trimmed away if it is inclined to get tangled under the saddle and numnah.
g. Removing the feathers at the back of the horse's legs will

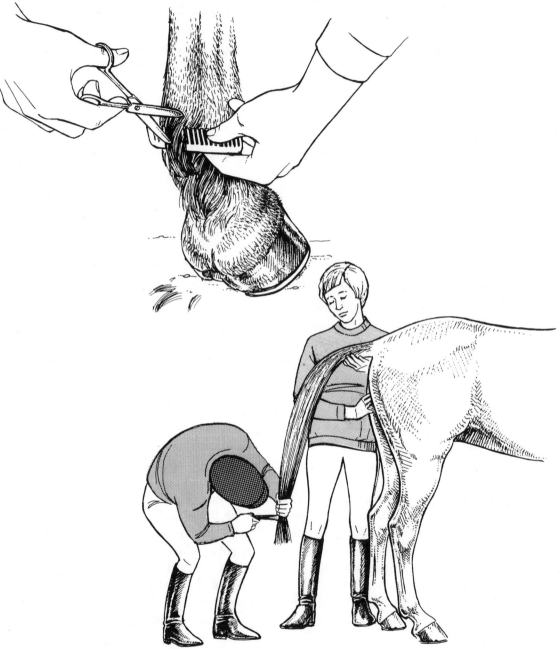

Trimming the heels and tail

improve its appearance and make it easier to keep the lower limbs clean. With a comb, comb the hair upwards, then trim the hair away level with the comb. This leaves a smooth finish.

h. To trim the end of the tail, first check the required length by asking an assistant to place a hand under the dock, lifting the tail to simulate the position in which the horse will carry it when moving. Then trim the bottom of the tail parallel to the ground, so that it hangs approximately 12 cm (4¾ in) below the point of the hock.

i. Some owners prefer not to trim any areas, particularly if they have a native pony, as these ponies are always shown in their natural state.   (30 minutes)

2. Pulling Manes and Tails

Manes

a. Manes are pulled to make them neat, tidy, easy to manage and short and thin enough to plait.

b. The hair will come out more easily when the horse is warm and the pores are open.

c. The hair should be removed over a period of several days, otherwise the horse will become sore and irritable.

d. Comb the mane to remove tangles. Hold a few of the long hairs between thumb and finger, while pushing back the shorter hairs with the comb. Wrap the long hairs around the comb, then give the comb a quick tug. The long hairs should come out by the roots.

e. Work gradually up and down the mane, removing the long hairs and trying to keep the mane level.

f. The forelock is pulled in the same way.

Tails

a. Tails are pulled to give the top a neat appearance, which also helps to show off the hind quarters to their best advantage.

b. If the horse has not had its tail pulled before, it may kick if it finds the process uncomfortable. Stand the horse with its hind quarters backed up to its stable door, while you stand on the other side for protection.

c. Remove the hairs gradually over a period of days.

d. Use comb and fingers to remove a few hairs at a time (in the same way as pulling the mane) from either side of the dock.

e. Work from the top, approximately 18–20 cm (7–7¾ in) down each side.

f. Finish by putting on a tail bandage for a short period of time. This will encourage the hairs to lie flat.   (15 minutes)

3. Plaiting

The Mane

a. A short, well-pulled mane will make plaiting easier.

b. You will need needle, thread and scissors or plaiting bands, a stool to stand on, water and water brush to damp the mane and a comb.

c. Plaiting bands and thread can be obtained in different colours to suit your horse.

d. Never plait with needle and thread while the horse is standing on bedding. If you drop the needle it will be lost, which will necessitate the removal of the whole bed.

e. Through trial and error, you will discover how much mane to take for each plait. As a rough guide, use the width of your mane comb to measure each section.

f. Using plaiting bands, divide the mane into even bunches. The number of plaits will depend upon the length of the horse's neck, the size of each plait and the thickness of the mane.

g. Push the comb into the mane to keep the loose hair out of the way.

h. Start at the poll and work back towards the withers. Damp the first section of mane, then divide into three even sections and plait to the end. Keep the plait tight.

J.A.Allen & Co.Ltd.
The Horseman's Publisher

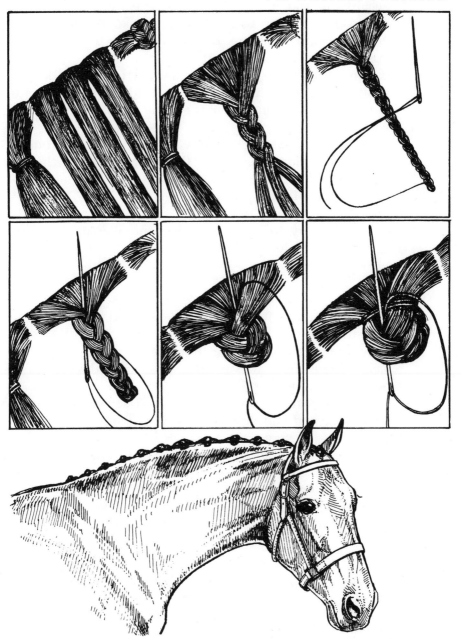

Plaiting the mane

i. Secure the end of the plait with a plaiting band, or with thread. Use the thread doubled with a knot in the end.

j. If using bands, roll up the plait and secure as tightly as possible with a second band.

k. If using thread, fold the plait in half, by taking the bottom up to the top and stitch this together. Fold again and then once more (depending on the length of the plait), securing the fold with a stitch each time.

l. Finish off by winding the thread once or twice around the base of the plait, then draw the thread through the whole plait and cut the thread off.

m. Do not trim off any protruding wisps of hair. This will ruin the mane, leaving it uneven and spiky when not plaited.

n. It is customary to have an uneven number of plaits in the mane plus one forelock plait.

The Tail

a. Brush and comb the tail, then thoroughly damp the hair to be plaited.

b. Take a small section of hair from the top at either side, and a small section from the middle, giving you three sections to begin plaiting with.

c. Progress down the dock, taking small sections of hair from either side and adding them into your plait.

e. Keep the plait very tight.

f. When you reach the end of the dock make one long plait from the remaining middle section of hair.

g. Secure the end of the plait with thread or a plaiting band. Double it up to make a loop, securing it with thread or plaiting bands at the end of the main dock plait.

(30 minutes)

4. Finishing Touches

a. Quarter markings can be applied by placing a stencil on the coat then body brushing the hair at right angles to its normal direction of growth. When the stencil is removed, an attractive

J.A. Allen & Co. Ltd.
The Horseman's Publisher

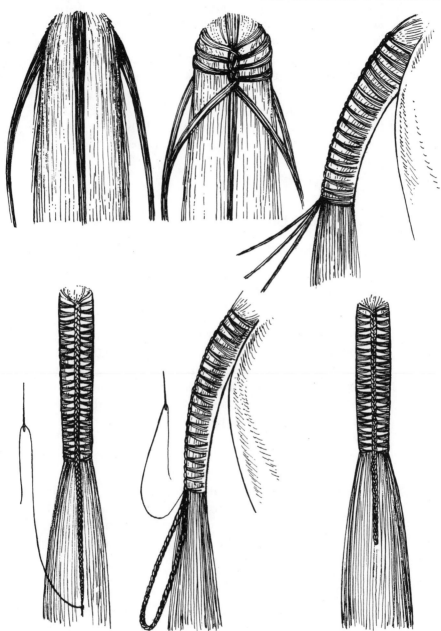

Plaiting the tail

pattern is left on the coat. This can also be done without a stencil. You can practise making different patterns with a body brush or comb.

b. To darken black skin around the eyes and muzzle and add an attractive gloss, a thin layer of baby oil can be applied.

c. Rub chalk into white legs. This is especially effective if the horse has thickly feathered legs.

d. Hoof oil gives a shine to the wall of the foot.   (10 minutes)

5. Loading and Unloading

Before fetching the horse, the students can inspect the horse box and trailer.

Preparation

a. Check that the vehicles are roadworthy, for example, road tax, brakes, oil, water, tyres, lights, connections, etc.

b. Park the vehicle in a safe location for loading; for example, an enclosed area from which the horse cannot escape. Use a quiet area with as few distractions as possible. An inexperienced horse may distrust the loading process and attempt to break loose. Distractions may cause the horse to back out of the box or to refuse to go in at all.

c. The ramp must rest firmly and not rock on uneven ground.

d. Both ramp and internal flooring must be non-slip. Rubber matting is ideal. This can be lifted out and washed clean periodically. At the same time, check that the floor underneath is sound and not showing any signs of rotting. Alternatively, straw will provide a good surface, but must be cleaned out frequently.

e. The inside of the box must be free from any protrusions that might cause an injury if leant against or knocked into.

f. Partitions, breast bars and doors must be completely secure.

g. Check that there is string on the tie up rings.

h. Remove loose items, such as buckets, which might move or rattle and become entangled with or frighten the horse.

i. If the horse is likely to be difficult, park the box alongside a wall or hedge. This will help to guide the horse up the ramp. It is also helpful to park the box with its rear towards a slope or bank. When the ramp is let down it will rest on the slope, making it level or nearly so. With less of a slope, the horse will walk in with more confidence.

j. Horses may feel claustrophobic about entering the box. To help, open any front doors of a trailer, push partitions to one side and make the compartment as airy and light as possible.

Loading

Having parked and prepared the box:

a. The horse, clothed for travelling, should be led out with a bridle over the top of its head collar and rope. A bridle gives you more control when leading. Once in the box, the bridle can be slipped off, leaving the head collar to tie the horse up with.

b. The leader must wear gloves, hard hat and strong footwear for protection. It may also be helpful to carry a stick. A quick tap may be all it takes to encourage a hesitant horse.

c. The horse should be led at a purposeful walk straight towards the ramp.

d. An assistant must be available to put up the ramp and also to help if the horse is reluctant to go in. Take care never to stand directly behind a ramp, as it may fall on you if the horse rushes backwards. Two assistants are needed for safe opening and closing of heavy ramps.

e. Always keep looking straight ahead. Never look back towards the horse, even if it stops. You will only discourage forward activity.

f. Once in, hold the horse while the breaching strap is fastened and the ramp or partition is locked in place. The horse is now secure and can be tied up with a quick-release knot.

The Difficult Loader

If the horse refuses to enter the box, there are several ways to encourage it. Different tactics work with different horses. Remember to build up the horse's confidence and do not scare it. All handlers should wear protective clothing.

a. An assistant can stand inside the box and offer a small bucket of feed. Allow the horse a mouthful of feed each time it progresses a few steps.

b. Two assistants can hold a lunge line or soft rope around the horse's hind quarters, just above its hocks. Pressure is applied as the assistants walk forward on either side of the horse. This encourages the horse to walk forward. Take great care not to let the horse become entangled in the line.

c. Some horses suddenly gain confidence if each of their feet is picked up in turn and placed a little further up the ramp. In effect you are moving the horse's legs for it.

d. More experienced but stubborn characters will often respond to a quick tap with a whip on their hind quarters or a quick prod with the brush end of a yard broom.

e. Load a well-behaved and experienced horse into the box first. This may encourage the other horse to go in.

f. Whatever happens, it is vital that the leader should keep the horse straight. If the horse understands that it cannot escape around the side of the box, it will eventually go forward.

g. Reward the horse with feed once it is inside and secure.

Unloading

a. Untie the horse before the breaching strap is undone, the ramp let down or the partition opened.

b. If the horse is likely to be difficult, slip on a bridle for greater control.

c. With a box or trailer designed for the horse to walk out forwards, simply encourage it to walk slowly. Allow it to stop and take in its surroundings if it wants to. Keep it straight to prevent it from hitting its hips on the side of the box or slipping off the edge of the ramp.

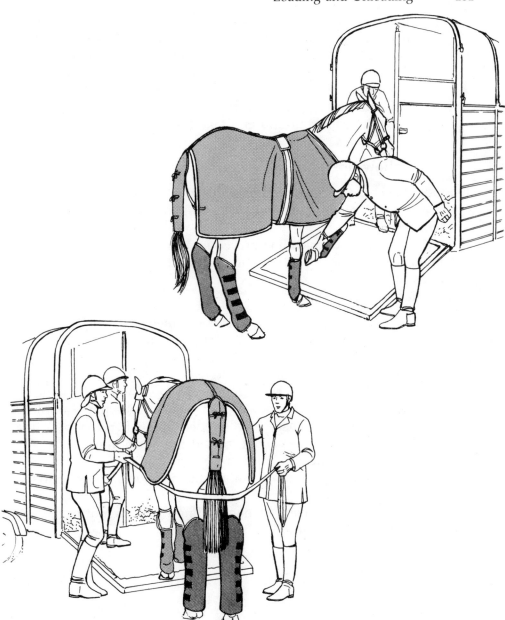

*If a horse refuses to load, there are several ways to encourage it —
placing a foreleg on the ramp may give the horse confidence; a lunge
rein behind the horse may help to push it forward*

    d. If you are using a rear-unload trailer, the horse's main problem is not being able to see what it is backing out onto. Assistants should stand on either side of the ramp and place a hand on the horse's hind quarters to guide it straight and reassure it.

    e. The horse may try to turn around, which will make it particularly inclined to come out crooked. Once it can see where it is, allow it to look around and take everything in. (45 minutes)

Follow-up Work

1. Students should be watched, helped and corrected while practising the art of trimming, mane and tail pulling and plaiting on a variety of horses.
2. As the loading and unloading procedure can be hazardous, students should be given the opportunity to observe, then assist, as frequently as possible, in order to gain experience.
3. Question and answer:

    a. What areas of the horse can be trimmed and why?

    b. Why are some horses' manes and tails pulled?

    c. Why shouldn't a horse be plaited, using needle and thread, when standing on bedding?

    d. What finishing touches can you use to show off the horse?

    e. What vehicle checks should be made before starting a journey?

    f. What do you consider when deciding where to park the vehicle that you are about to load the horse into?

    g. Why do you need an assistant when loading?

    h. How can you encourage a horse that is reluctant to go into the box?

    i. What do you consider when leading the horse out of the box forwards/backwards?

16 Clipping

Time

1 hour 30 minutes

Resources

a. Clipping machine.
b. Selection of horses with a variety of clips.
c. Horse and area suitable for clipping demonstration.
d. Handouts.
e. OHP.

Location

Lecture room, then stable yard.

Preparation

a. Put the clipping machine and blades in the lecture room.
b. Select horses with different clips and tie them up in a safe area.
c. Select and prepare the horse and area for the clipping demonstration.
d. Copy the correct number of handouts.
e. Set up the OHP and drawings of the different clips.

Aim

- To teach the reasons for clipping, how to prepare the horse, area and machine and how to clip.

Objective

- To improve the students' understanding of safe and effective procedures for clipping.

Start off in the lecture room.

1. Reasons for Clipping

- By removing all or part of a thick winter coat, a horse can continue to work without the distress caused by becoming hot and sweaty. This enables us to keep the horse fit.
- The horse will cool and dry off quickly after work. This helps to prevent chills and is labour saving.
- It is easier to keep a clipped horse clean and to spot the first signs of heat and swelling, etc. This, in turn, can help to prevent disease.
- Clipping can improve the horse's appearance.   (5 minutes)

2. Preparing the Horse for Clipping

a. Clipper blades will not run smoothly through a dirty coat. The horse should preferably be stabled and groomed thoroughly for several days before clipping. Wearing a light rug will also help to keep the coat clean.

b. If the horse is not familiar with the clippers, try to stand it next to a well-behaved horse while it is being clipped. This will help the first horse to get used to the noise.

c. Familiarise the horse with the clipping machine by resting it (switched off) against its coat. Move the clippers over the horse's body, giving the horse a chance to see the machine and electric cable.

d. When the horse is relaxed, with the machine switched off, stand away from it and turn the clippers on. Reassure the horse, then approach and rest the clippers against its shoulder without actually clipping. Again move the clippers over the coat.

e. It may be necessary to introduce the clippers over a period of several days. Once the horse is confident, you will be able to begin clipping.

f. Plait the horse's mane and bandage the tail to keep them out of the way.

g. Have a blanket ready to place over the newly clipped areas, in order to keep the horse warm.

h. The horse's coat must be completely dry.

i. Outline the type of clip to be followed by drawing on the horse's coat with chalk or saddle soap. (A brightly coloured lipstick is excellent.) Check that the saddle patch, blanket, etc., are drawn the same size and depth on each side.

j. For a hunter clip, draw around the horse's usual saddle to make a saddle patch outline. If the horse wears both dressage and jumping saddles, combine the two by following the straight cut front of the dressage saddle and the shorter flap length of the jumping saddle.   (15 minutes)

3. Preparation and Choice of the Clipping Area

a. To see clearly what and where you are clipping, plenty of daylight is needed. At the same time, you need to be prepared for poor weather, so good electric lighting is also required.

b. An area that is sheltered from wind and rain is essential. The horse should not be subjected to draughts and the machinery must be kept dry.

c. The flooring must be non-slip. A purpose-built area with rubber matting on the floor is ideal. This provides a non-slip surface that can be cleaned easily and will provide some degree of insulation in the case of an electrical fault. Alternatively, a thin layer of straw can be laid on the stable floor.

d. A power point is needed, with a circuit breaker for safety.

e. It is helpful to have a ceiling hook for the electric cable. This will keep the cable off the floor where it may otherwise be stepped on by the horse.   (10 minutes)

4. The Clipping Machine and its Care

Use the clipping machine to demonstrate the relevant parts and how to put on and remove the blades.

a. Check that the clippers are in good working order. They should be serviced by an expert after each season's use.

b. Make sure the cable is intact, with no splits in the outer cover and no loose connections at either plug or machine end.

c. Clippers should be fitted with a wrist strap for safety. Put your hand through the strap, then hold the clippers. If the horse moves suddenly and you lose your grip, the clippers should end up swinging from your wrist rather than crashing to the ground.

d. The whole machine must be very clean. Check that the air vents are not clogged with hair.

e. The blades must be very sharp and will need to be resharpened after, approximately, one full clip or two blanket clips. Select coarse blades for long thick coats and finer blades for short fine coats.

f. Secure the blades and adjust the tension according to the manufacturer's instructions. (Approximate guide for tension: turn the tension screw until you feel some resistance, then make one and a half more turns.) If the tension is too tight, the machine will quickly overheat; if too loose, the blades will not clip.

g. The machine needs to be well oiled (point out the oiling points) using clipper oil only. Thicker oils will reduce the efficiency of the machine and eventually stop it from working. Apply oil to the blades.

h. Plug in and switch on. Allow the machine to run for a few moments while the oil works in. The clippers are now ready for use.

i. During clipping, test the flat blade against the back of your hand every fifteen minutes or so. If it is getting hot, it will scorch the horse, so then you need to stop and allow the blades to cool. A variety of cooling fluids are available for spraying onto the blades.

j. While the blades are cooling, remove them from the clippers and clean away all the loose hair. You will need a soft brush and a cloth with which to keep the air vents, blades and head of the clippers clean.

k. During a full clip, you will probably stop approximately four to six times to cool the blades, clean the machine and reoil it.

l. After clipping, remove and clean the blades. Store them in oiled cloth or paper, to prevent rusting. Thoroughly clean the machine and wrap the head in oiled cloth. Store in a dry place.   (20 minutes)

5. Different Types of Clip

Start in the lecture room, then move to the stable yard to look at horses.

- Full clip − All the coat is removed. A good clip to improve the appearance of thick-coated horses. Used for fit, stabled horses in hard work.

- Hunter clip − The legs and saddle patch are left on, the rest of the coat is removed. Used for hunters as the leg hair protects the horse from thorns etc. in undergrowth, while the saddle patch protects the back from the saddle and a rider who may stay mounted for several hours. Suitable for all stabled, fit horses in hard work.

- Blanket clip − The hair is left on the legs and in a blanket shape over the horse's back. Suitable for stabled horses that feel the cold, suffer from azoturia or are in medium work.

- Chaser clip − The hair is removed from beneath a sloping line that runs from the stifle up to the poll. The hair is left on the legs. This is a variation of the blanket clip, used for the same reasons. It is also useful if the horse is reluctant to be clipped around the hind legs.

- Trace clip − The hair is removed below a horizontal line running from mid-thigh to the point of the shoulder, including a strip up the underside of the horse's neck. The hair is left on the legs. This is suitable for working horses kept at grass in a New Zealand rug.

J.A.Allen & Co.Ltd.
The Horseman's Publisher

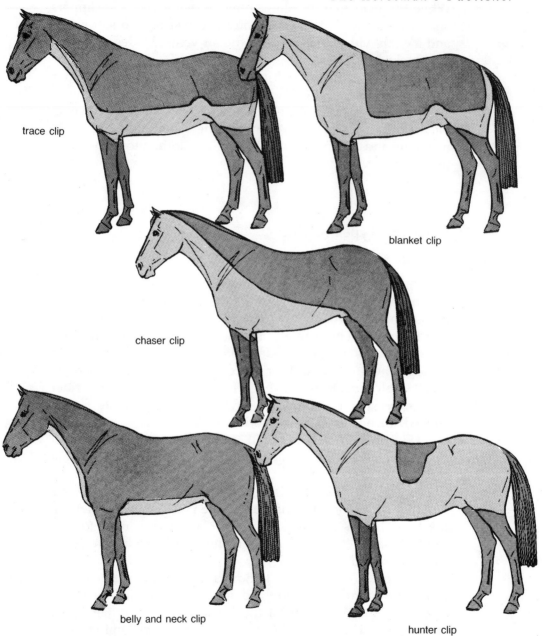

trace clip

blanket clip

chaser clip

belly and neck clip

hunter clip

Different types of clip

- Belly and neck clip − This clip has various different names and involves removing a small amount of hair from under the belly and the underside of the neck. It is suitable for grass-kept ponies that may not be rugged up but are inclined to sweat when worked.
- There are many variations on the above clips. The height of blanket, chaser and trace clips may vary. Owners may alter the style in order to improve the horse's appearance. For example, a high leg line will make the legs look longer.
- The face hair may be left on with any clip if the horse is reluctant to have its head clipped. Alternatively, half the face hair can be removed, by following the vertical line made by the cheekpiece of the bridle.   (15 minutes)

6. How to Clip

Using the horse prepared for clipping, demonstrate the following:

a. The hair removed will stick to your clothes, so wear overalls and a head scarf or hat. It is also advisable to wear rubber-soled footwear in case of an electrical fault.

b. The shoulder is usually the best place to start. It is a smooth, easily accessible area, not ticklish and a safe distance from the hind legs. Providing the horse relaxes after the first few strokes, you can then progress to any part of the body.

c. The difficult parts of the process are making smooth, straight, even lines and obtaining a neat finish around areas like the elbows and head. If the horse is relaxed, tackle these areas first, while you and the horse are at your most patient.

d. Press the clippers flat against the horse's skin and run them into the coat against the lie of the hair. By making long, smooth strokes, you will gain a smoother finish.

e. Each time the lie of the hair changes, for example, when you meet a whorl, you will need to change the direction of the clippers so that you continue to clip against the lie of the hair.

f. In order not to pinch the horse, you will need to use your spare hand to smooth the horse's skin, especially in areas like the neck and behind the elbow where the skin wrinkles easily.

g. If removing the hair from the quarters, make a neat finish at the top of the tail by forming a small triangle.

h. When clipping the neck, take care not to remove any of the mane, as this will result in unsightly tufts as it grows out.

i. It is better not to give the horse a haynet. Each time it pulls hay, the movement will make it difficult for you to keep the clippers steady.

j. It is useful to have an assistant to hold up each of the front legs in turn as you clip around the elbows. It may also be necessary to hold up a leg to encourage the horse to stay still while a ticklish area is clipped.

k. You will probably need a stool to stand on in order to reach some areas.

l. Don't forget to check the heat of the blades frequently, keep brushing them clean and apply more oil or cooling spray at regular intervals.

m. Start clipping early in the day. This will allow you plenty of daylight hours if the horse proves difficult. You need to complete the clip within one day to avoid it looking patchy.

(15 minutes)

Further Points

1. Most horses have their first clip in September/October, when the winter coat is well through. However, if your horse is just starting a fitness programme at this time of year, leave the coat on for warmth until you have completed the walking stage.

   You may need to reclip two or three times during the winter. Plan the last clip for January/February. By the time this clip has grown out, the winter coat will be ready to moult.

2. An experienced clipper will complete a full or hunter clip in 45–60 minutes, providing the horse is well behaved. Difficult horses can take all day to complete.

3. Many horses behave well until it comes to clipping their heads. It is probably the noise that worries them or it may

be the vibration. Some will stand quietly if twitched. Alternatively, they may tolerate the type of clippers used for dogs. These are small and tend to purr, which is less frightening. If a horse is very frightened of clipping in general, you can arrange for your vet to sedate the horse.

4. Immediately after clipping, rub down the clipped areas with a hot damp towel. This will open the pores and lift off grease and loose hair.   (10 minutes)

Follow-up Work

1. Students should assist an experienced clipper as often as possible and be allowed to practise clipping under their guidance, starting with easy areas.
2. Question and answer:

   a. Why do we clip horses?
   b. How do you prepare a horse for clipping?
   c. What sort of area would you like for clipping in?
   d. What care and maintenance does the clipping machine need?
   e. What different types of clip are there, and when is each type most likely to be used?

17 Safety

Time

1 hour 15 minutes

Resources

a. OHP.
b. Heavy object; for example, feed sack/hay bale.
c. Haynet and tie up ring.
d. Yard with fire-fighting equipment.
e. Handouts.

Location

Lecture room and stable yard.

Preparation

a. Set up the OHP in the lecture room.
b. Put the hay bale/feed sack and haynet in an undercover area of the yard.
c. Note all fire fighting points on the yard.
d. Copy handouts.

Aims

- To teach the students safe procedures when working on the yard and riding in the countryside.
- To teach the students the correct procedure to follow in the event of a fire or an accident.

Objective

- To increase awareness of safety and to help prevent accidents.

While all previous and subsequent lectures have included points on the safe way of carrying out various tasks, the following covers some more general points of safety.

1. Clothing for Working around Horses

In the lecture room.

- Strong footwear, to protect you if trodden on etc., is essential. The ideal would be boots with steel toe caps but these are rarely worn by anyone but farriers. Leather boots give good protection. The soles must provide good grip.
- All clothing must allow freedom of movement. However, if too loose and baggy, it can catch on things or flap and frighten the horses.
- Bright colours may also be frightening and should be avoided.
- Gloves should be worn whenever possible. By preventing wounds and scratches to your hands, you avoid problems like tetanus and Weil's disease.
- All jewellery should be avoided. Rings, bracelets, earrings, etc., can easily get caught up and cause serious injury to the wearer.
- Long hair can also get caught and is better tied back or worn under a hat.
- A hard hat should be worn when handling problem or young horses.
- For riding, a hard hat of BSI Standard 6473 or 4472 must always be worn. Footwear must have a small heel, not a wedge type, to prevent the foot from slipping through the stirrup and becoming stuck. The sole should be fairly smooth, as deep ridges may also cause feet to get stuck.

(10 minutes)

2. General Safety around the Yard

Keeping the yard tidy is the most important step towards safety. Any item left lying around can become a hazard. The tidying up process is usually called "setting fair".

On the yard, point out and demonstrate the following:

- A bag or bin can be provided for any string removed from hay and straw bales.
- Yard tools need hooks to hang from or a specific storage room.
- The yard surface should be non-slip and kept free from debris by regular sweeping. This will also remove hay and straw that could become a fire hazard. In winter, grit or salt should be spread on ice to maintain a safe surface.
- Grooming kit, tack, clothing, buckets, etc., must always be put away. Haynets pose a particular hazard for both horse and human if left lying around.
- When a full haynet is given to a horse, it should be tied up bearing in mind how low it will hang when empty. Pull the haynet up as high as possible, then draw the string through the bottom of the haynet and pull it back up to the top. Tie with a quick-release knot, then turn the net so that the knot is hidden at the back where it is less likely to be pulled undone by the horse.
- Yard work often involves moving heavy objects. This can be hazardous if not tackled correctly. Always enlist the help of a fellow worker where possible. Trolleys, wheelbarrows, etc., should be used to move hay bales, feed sacks and other items, rather than trying to carry them.
- When lifting, try to keep your back straight. Bend your knees rather than bending at the waist and push up using your thigh muscles, rather than pulling up with your back muscles.
- Keep weights balanced; for example, carry two water buckets, one in each hand, rather than one, which will pull you sideways.
- Carry heavy weights close to your body to help you to maintain balance.

incorrect

correct

Lifting a heavy weight

- General maintenance is essential. For example, door bolts need to work smoothly; electrical fittings must be secure and well insulated; holes in the yard or buildings need quick repair, and so on.   (20 minutes)

3. Fire Precautions

Start in the lecture room. Use the OHP to display the main points. Move on to the yard and point out fire points, hazards, etc.

   a. Prevention is best, so keep the yard tidy (as mentioned above) to prevent the spread of fire if it occurs.
   b. A muck heap can get very hot and may self-ignite, so position it well away from buildings.
   c. Hay, straw and shavings should be stored away from the stables.

d. Taps, hoses and troughs (keep them full) can all be used to fight a fire.
e. Arrange for a fire officer to visit. He or she will advise on fire extinguishers, telling you how many are needed, where to put them and what type to have.
f. Put up one or more fire notices. These should have white lettering on a green background, and read as follows:

IN THE EVENT OF A FIRE
1. Raise the alarm.
2. Move horses to safety.
3. Dial 999 for fire brigade.
4. Fight the fire.

After each point, details are required:
- The location of the fire alarm.
- Designated place of safety for the horses.
- Location of the nearest telephone.
- Location of fire fighting equipment.

g. Put NO SMOKING notices around the yard and provide buckets full of sand in which cigarettes can be extinguished.
h. All workers should know and practise the yard fire drill.

(15 minutes)

4. Riding Out and the Country Code

In the lecture room.

There are various rules of safe conduct that help to maintain a good relationship between riders and other countryside users.

a. If on horseback when passing walkers or other riders, always walk and give them a wide berth. If you approach them from the rear, make your presence known. It is, in any case, only polite to say "Good morning", etc.
b. Do not ride on private land without permission. Keep to bridleways and other areas designated for horses.
c. Ride around the edges of fields with crops in them.
d. Do not ride through livestock. Walk around them, giving them a wide berth.

e. Leave gates as you find them, unless it is obvious that someone has forgotten to secure a gate and livestock are escaping, in which case inform the farmer.
f. Be aware of people, dogs, etc., in gardens. When hidden from your horse's view, behind a hedge or fence, any noise or movement could cause your horse to shy into the road.
g. Never trot around blind corners on roads or tracks. There could be any number of unforeseen hazards, so be prepared and slow to a walk.
h. Avoid busy roads whenever possible, and take the riding and road safety test.   (10 minutes)

5. Accident Procedure

It is advisable for everyone to have first-aid training, whatever their occupation. The following is the procedure to take in the event of an accident, rather than how to administer first aid.

a. First, remain calm, as it is important to think clearly.
b. Make the situation safe. If someone has been kicked, move the horse away. If someone has fallen off, halt the rest of the ride and send a person to catch the loose horse. Each situation will be a little different, so use common sense.
c. Go to the injured person. Reassure them and tell them to keep still.

If Conscious

d. Encourage them to breath deeply and calmly. (They may be winded and panicking about getting air.)
e. Ask them if there is any pain. Can they move their fingers and toes?
f. Make a mental note of what they say; it will be helpful information to give the doctor or ambulance staff, should they be needed.
g. Keep talking to the person. If they appear to be talking non-sense, they may have concussion and will need to be taken to a doctor.

h. If they cannot move their fingers or toes or have pain in neck, back or limbs, do not move them. Ask for an ambulance to be called. Keep them warm with a blanket. Do not try to remove hat or boots, etc.

i. Obvious bleeding should be stemmed by applying light pressure with a handkerchief or clean pad.

j. If they feel fine and want to get up, allow them to do so on their own. Stand near in case they feel faint and need support. Do not allow them to remount if you feel there is any chance they may faint. Allow them to walk for a while.

If Unconscious

k. Check there is no blockage in the mouth that may prevent breathing and carefully loosen any tight clothing around the neck.

l. Do not move the person. Send for an ambulance. Anyone who has been unconscious must be examined by a doctor in case of skull damage.

m. Keep talking to them; this may help to bring them round. Keep them warm.

n. Remain calm and also reassure the rest of your ride as soon as possible. Once the injured person has been taken to hospital, you may resume the work, hack or lesson.

Further Points

a. Be prepared for accidents. Have the telephone number of your local doctor and vet clearly displayed by the telephone. Dial 999 for an ambulance. Have a first-aid kit on the yard and one that can be taken out when hacking.

b. If you have a pay phone, keep money for emergencies in an obvious place beside the phone. When hacking, take money for the phone.

c. If an accident occurs on the road, someone should be posted on either side to redirect traffic. With luck, there will be a motorist with a car phone who will be able to summon help.

It is obviously important to catch the loose horse as it may cause further accidents.

On return home, you should fill in a British Horse Society Accident Report From. This helps the Road Safety Development Officer of the BHS to compile statistics on road accidents involving horses.

d. If an accident involves injury to human and horse, take care of the human first but attend to the horse or send someone else to do so as soon as possible.

e. After any accident, write the details in the yard accident book.   (20 minutes)

Follow-up Work

1. Observe students demonstrating their understanding of correct clothing by wearing suitable clothes for their daily work on the yard.
2. Students should be observed setting fair the yard to show they understand the importance of tidiness.
3. Observe students to check that they follow the correct procedures for lifting weights and tying up haynets.
4. Hold regular fire drills. If the procedure becomes second nature to each person, they will all react more swiftly and calmly if there is a fire.
5. Question and answer:

    a. What clothing should be avoided, and why, when working with horses?
    b. Why is it important to keep the yard tidy?
    c. What four main headings should appear on a fire notice?
    d. Explain some rules that should be observed when riding in the countryside.
    e. Explain the procedure to take in the event of an accident.

18 Stables and their Construction

Time

1 hour 30 minutes

Resources

a. Yard with a selection of stables, building materials and fittings.
b. OHP.

Location

Lecture room and stable yard.

Preparation

a. Note the main features of the yard that will be helpful to your lecture.
b. Set up the OHP and prepare acetates with drawings of dimensions, roof lines, etc.

Aim

- To teach students the main features to be aware of with regard to stable construction.

Objective

- To enable students to assess the suitability of a building to be used for stabling.

1. The Site, Drainage and Flooring

In the lecture room, use the OHP to illustrate where appropriate.

Site

a. If you are able to choose the site, the stables should be positioned with their backs to the prevailing wind.
b. Choose an area that should drain well. If at the bottom of a dip, the stables and drains may flood in wet weather.
c. Large trees too close to the building may pose a problem in stormy weather if a branch or the whole tree falls.
d. Other considerations include accessibility for vehicles, electricity and water.

Drainage and Flooring

a. Drains are generally laid to take all water away from the stables towards the rear.
b. When the floor is laid, a slight slope towards the front or rear is incorporated to aid drainage. If the slope drains into a front channel it is visible and easy to keep clear. However, as horses often stand at the front of their boxes, this may lead to them standing in the wettest area. If the slope drains into a back channel it will be less visible and may become blocked, but the horse will usually be standing in a drier area. Each individual must weigh up the pros and cons.
c. Drainage channels and covers must be swept clean daily.
d. Concrete, with little ridges on the surface for grip, is the most commonly used flooring. The concrete is laid a metre or so larger than the floor area needed. This allows for hard dry standing immediately outside the boxes.   (15 minutes)

2. The Structure

Walls

• Wooden walls are frequently used and can be purchased in sections ready to erect.

- Brickwork, one or two bricks high (or more), is put down as a base for the wooden structure. This helps to prevent rotting and invasion by rats.
- The higher the brick base, the more expensive the structure becomes. For this reason, complete brick-built boxes are not often erected these days.
- Breeze blocks are a cheaper alternative and may be used as a compromise between brick and wood. The advantages of brick/breeze block over wood are that they are more durable and also fire proof.
- A small hole must be incorporated in the base of the wall for drainage.
- Walls should be approximately 240 cm (nearly 8 ft) high to the eaves, to allow for head room.
- Walls and doors need to be lined with kicking boards. This will protect both the outer walls and the horse from each other. Kicking boards also provide insulation and strengthen the walls. They are usually 120 cm (4 ft) high.

Dimensions

- A box 300 × 300 cm (10 × 10 ft) would provide enough room for a pony up to 14.2 h.h.
- 300 × 360 cm or 360 × 360 cm (10 × 12 ft or 12 × 12 ft) provides enough room for a 14.2−16.2 h.h. horse.
- 360 × 420 cm or 420 × 420 cm (12 × 14 ft or 14 × 14 ft) would be a suitable size for a horse over 16.2 h.h.
- Boxes for very large horses, or for foaling, should be 480 × 480 cm (16 × 16 ft).
- Doorways should be 120 cm (4 ft) wide, with a bottom door height suitable for the size of horse. Horses 14.2 h.h. and above will usually have a bottom door 120 cm (4 ft) high, with a top door of 90 cm (3 ft), making a total doorway height of 210 cm (7 ft).
- Pony boxes will have lower bottom doors and will not require as much head room in the doorway.

Roof

- A pitched roof gives more head room and air space inside the box and also drains well.
- The roof should overhang the front of the boxes by approximately 90 cm (3 ft). This will keep the horses dry and give shade when they have their heads over the door.
- Air vents may be put in the roof to aid good circulation of air.
- Roofing felt provides an attractive and relatively inexpensive roof covering. However, its insulation properties are poor and it is not fireproof. As it is inclined to expand and contract in hot and cold weather, cracks will gradually appear, leading to leaks.
- Slate is more expensive, but is attractive, insulates well and is fireproof. However, it does crack easily.
- Tiles are more expensive still, but are strong, attractive and have excellent insulation properties that keep the stables warm in winter and cool in summer. They are also fireproof.
- Corrugated sheets of plastic, iron and a mix containing asbestos can provide a cheaper form of roofing. Iron is the worst of the three. It is hot in summer, cold in winter and very noisy when it rains. Plastic is a useful addition to all types of roof as it provides an extra source of light. The asbestos mix is fireproof and provides reasonable insulation. Obtainable in large sheets, it is quick to erect but a whole sheet will need replacing if a crack appears.   (30 minutes)

3. Fittings

- Stable doors, particularly the top door which is rarely closed, need hooks to secure them when open.
- When closed, they need strong bolts to secure them. On the bottom door use a bolt design that your horse cannot open at the top, and a kick bolt at the bottom.
- A metal strip along the top of the lower door can prevent the horse from chewing the wood. The upper part of the door frame may also be covered with metal to prevent chewing.

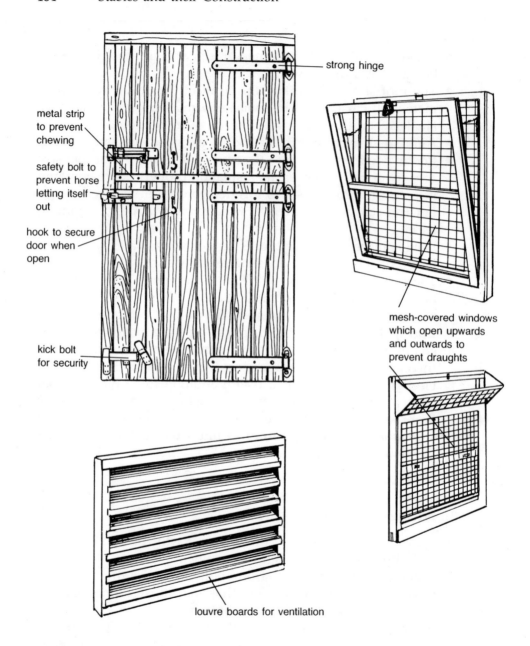

strong hinge

metal strip
to prevent
chewing

safety bolt to
prevent horse
letting itself
out

hook to secure
door when
open

kick bolt
for security

mesh-covered windows
which open upwards
and outwards to
prevent draughts

louvre boards for ventilation

Safe stable fittings

- Windows should be located on the same side of the box as the door. This prevents through draughts, while providing light and fresh air.
- Windows that hinge at the bottom to open outwards prevent draughts. They should be covered with a wire mesh and be glazed with wired safety glass.
- Louvre boards can be used to provide further draught-free ventilation, and are usually positioned fairly high up on the wall.
- Tie-up rings should be positioned towards the front of the box. Then, when the horse is tied up, you will be able to enter the box with the horse's head towards you, rather than its hind quarters. Fix the ring approximately at eye level.
- Further fittings, for example, automatic water bowl, hay rack, feed manger, are optional. If used, there should be no sharp edges and each item should be high enough to prevent the horse getting its legs caught.
- Strip lighting or bulbs can be used. Position these well above the horse's head height. They must also be covered to prevent shattered glass falling into the bed. The light switch should be outside the stable, out of the horse's reach. Obviously, all electrical wires must be well insulated and covered to keep them away from horses and protected from weather and rodent damage.   (15 minutes)

4. Converted Buildings

Many buildings are converted from their original use for use as stables. It is important to check that these conversions will provide a safe environment for the horse. Each situation will vary but the following points should be considered.

    a. Buildings and dividing walls must be strong enough to withstand being kicked and lent on by the horse. Badly built walls crumble and fall easily, while flimsy wood panels will splinter.

    b. There must always be plenty of head room in the doorway and inside the building. Old barns with low beams may not be suitable.

    c. Dividing walls that do not reach up to the ceiling must be high enough to stop the horses from reaching over into the neighbouring box.

    d. Check that there are no protrusions that could damage the horse; for example, old nails, hooks, etc.   (10 minutes)

Now take the students out into the yard and observe a variety of materials, fittings and structures.   (20 minutes)

Follow-up Work

1. Try to visit a number of different yards. Ask the students to point out all the good points about the buildings on each yard and then all the not-so-good points.
2. Question and answer:

    a. What points should be considered when choosing a site for stables?

    b. What box dimensions are suitable for
      i. A 14.2 h.h. pony;
      ii. A mare and foal;
      iii. A stable doorway?

    c. What different roofing materials are available?

    d. What are some of the pros and cons of various roofing materials?

    e. What fittings would you wish to have in your stable?

19   The Skeleton

Time

60 minutes

Resources

a. A full-size model, or real skeleton (if possible), of the horse.
b. A quiet, fit horse.
c. Handouts.
d. OHP.

Location

Lecture room and stable yard.

Preparation

a. Put the skeleton (or examples of bones and different joints) in the lecture room.
b. Select a slim, fit horse, which will make it relatively easy to locate the position of the bones under the skin and muscle.
c. Copy handouts.
d. Set up the OHP and prepare acetates to show how the skeleton protects internal organs, etc.

Aim

- To teach the students about the structure and uses of the skeleton.

Objective

- To help students to take better care of horses by improving their knowledge of internal structures.

Start in the lecture room.

1. Why We Need to Know about the Skeleton

a. By learning where the bones are located, we can avoid causing damage to the horse; for example, when wisping it is important to avoid bony areas.
b. If a horse receives an injury, we will know if that location may have involved a bone. This will help when deciding whether or not to call the vet.
c. Understanding the structure of the horse helps in the assessment of conformation, which, in turn, helps us to understand each horse's limitations.   (5 minutes)

2. Aspects to Note

Use the OHP and actual skeleton to point out the bones, joints and their functions, noting the following:

a. The skeleton is the structure or framework around which the body is built.
b. When the joints are used, the skeleton is mobile rather than rigid.
c. There are three types of joint:
   - Immovable joints – where bones fuse together, like those in the skull.
   - Slightly movable joints – where bones are not fused but movement is very limited, as in the backbone.
   - Freely movable joints – these divide into a further four types – plane, hinged, pivot, and ball and socket.

d. The skull protects the brain and parts of the ears, eyes and nasal passages. Along with the lower jaw bone, it also houses the teeth.

e. The bones of the backbone are called **vertebrae**. There is a channel through these vertebrae. The spinal cord runs along this channel and is protected by it.

f. The five **sacral vertebrae** are fused together.

g. The eighteen pairs of ribs which are attached to the **thoracic vertebrae** protect many of the internal organs, especially the lungs.

h. Eight pairs of ribs are "true" and ten pairs are "false". The "true" pairs attach directly to the **sternum**, as well as to the vertebrae, while the "false" pairs are attached to the vertebrae but are only attached to the sternum by cartilage.

i. The front limbs have no bony attachment to the rest of the skeleton. They are only joined by muscles, tendons and ligaments. (The horse does not have a collar bone.)

j. The **pelvis** is formed by a number of fused bones: the fused sacral vertebrae, **ilium**, **pubis** and **ischium**.

k. Some bones contain marrow, which is where blood cells are formed.

l. Cartilage is a smooth, flexible substance. While the horse is still growing, it can be found at the end of long bones, where it ossifies into bone. It is also found in joints, where, covering the surfaces of bones that meet, it prevents friction. Being flexible, it can help to give support, while allowing for movement; for example, the rings of cartilage in the trachea, and the cartilage that joins some of the ribs to the sternum.

m. Many bones have surface projections that aid the attachment of muscles; for example, the spinal processes of the vertebrae.

n. If we imagine the human as an animal on all fours, we can see that many of the horse's joints are equivalent to our own:
   - horse's stifle = human knee.
   - horse's hock = human heel.
   - horse's knee = human wrist.
   - horse's leg below the knee = human middle finger.

(25 minutes)

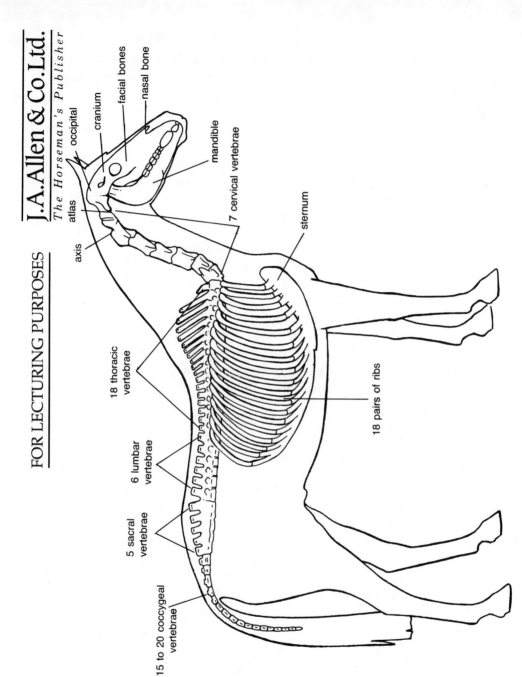

FOR LECTURING PURPOSES

occipital

cranium

facial bones

nasal bone

atlas

axis

mandible

7 cervical vertebrae

sternum

18 thoracic vertebrae

6 lumbar vertebrae

5 sacral vertebrae

18 pairs of ribs

15 to 20 coccygeal vertebrae

Axial skeleton (bones of the skull, spine, ribs and sternum)

scapula

humerus

radius

carpus

cannon

long pastern

short pastern

pedal bone

ulna

pisiform bone

splint bones

sesamoid bones

navicular bone

tibia

pelvis

femur

fibula

os calcis

tarsus

splint bones

cannon

sesamoid bones

long pastern

short pastern

navicular bone

pedal bone

Appendicular skeleton (bones of the limbs)

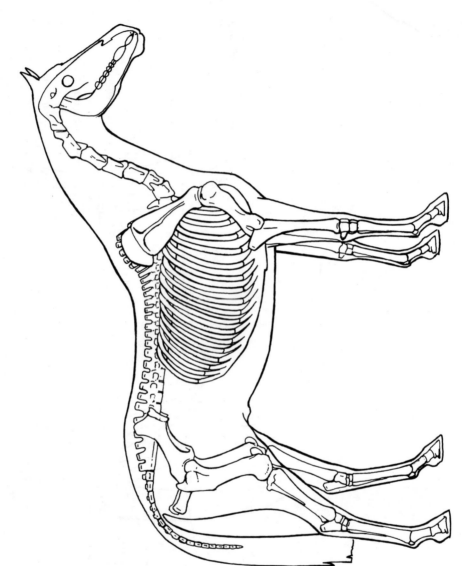

The whole skeleton

3. Practice

Now move to the stable yard. Using the selected horse and a diagram of the skeleton, outline where the bones lie under the skin and muscle.
Allow the students to take turns in pointing out where the bones lie.
(30 minutes)

Follow-up Work

1. Question and answer:

    a. Point out the location of the following on the horse:
      i. lumbar vertebrae;
      ii. sternum;
      iii. mandible, etc.
    b. How many cervical vertebrae are there?
    c. What do the ribs protect?
    d. Where, on the skeleton, would you find cartilage?
    e. What runs through the channel in the vertebrae?
    f. Why are some ribs called "true", and some "false"?
    g. Are the front limbs attached by bone to the rest of the skeleton?
    h. Which of the horse's joints are equivalent to our own?
    i. Does the horse have a collar bone?